英訳付き
ニッポンの名前図鑑
和食・年中行事

監修　服部幸應

An Illustrated Guide to
Japanese Cooking and
Annual Events

Editorial Supervisor　Hattori Yukio

淡交社

はじめに

蕎麦湯をつぐアノ容器は、なんていう名前？
「曲げわっぱ」って、どんなもの？
「門松」は英語でどのように説明したらいい？

日本に暮らしていても、意外に知らないモノ・コトが身の回りに多くあります。形を知っていても、名前がわからないモノ。名前を聞いても、どんな形か想像できないモノ。名前を知っていても、具体的に由来やいわれを説明できないコト。
近年、和の文化、特に「和食」が世界的に注目されているにもかかわらず、和食について人と話ができないのは、心もとないことです。また、外国人にも大人気の寿司を英語で説明できないのも、残念に思うときがあるかもしれません。
本書では、日本人として知っておきたい伝統的な「和食」「食器」「年中行事」にまつわるモノ・コトの名前を取り上げました。一般的に広く使われている名前を選び、解説をつけましたが、それらは全国共通ではない場合があります。特に年中行事はすべての地域に対応するわけではないことを、あらかじめご承知おきください。
さあ、これまで見過ごしてきた日本特有のモノ・コトを見つめ直しましょう。日本文化になじみのない方も、この本を通してニッポンの名前を知っていただければ幸いです。友人や外国の方にさらっと説明ができるなんて、少し誇らしくありませんか？

Introduction

What is that pot for serving *sobayu* called?
What exactly is a *magewappa*?
And how can I explain *kadomatsu* in English?

    Living in Japan, we find that there are many things around us we don't know. We know what some things look like, but cannot remember their names. Others we cannot even picture. And some things we can easily identify, but cannot explain their origins.

    Recently, Japanese culture, especially *washoku*, has attracted attention worldwide. As such, you might feel somewhat uneasy attempting to discuss *washoku* with people around you. Or, you might let yourself down when you are unable to explain what sushi is in English, despite its popularity overseas.

    This book is a collection of things related to traditional Japanese cooking, tableware and annual events. They are all things that one, as a Japanese person, would want to know. Although we have chosen names used most generally, they may not be common in all parts of Japan. Please note that annual events especially differ among regions.

    Now, let's reexamine the Japanese things that we have overlooked. For those of you who aren't familiar with Japanese culture, we hope that you will enjoy learning more through this book. Wouldn't it be wonderful if you could explain these things to your friends and to people all over the world?

目次　Contents

和食
JAPANESE COOKING

会席料理　Course Dishes

先付・sakizuke／付出し・tsukidashi
椀盛・wanmori／椀物・wanmono　　　　　　　　　　　12
向付・mukozuke／造り・tsukuri／刺身・sashimi
焼物・yakimono　　　　　　　　　　　　　　　　　　13
煮物・nimono／炊き合せ・takiawase　　　　　　　　　14
揚物・agemono　強肴・shiizakana／進肴・susumezakana　15
ご飯・gohan　止椀・tomewan　香の物・konomono　　　16
水菓子・mizugashi　甘味・kammi　　　　　　　　　　　17

定番料理　Classic Dishes

鯖の味噌煮・saba no miso-ni
金目鯛の煮付け・kimmedai no nitsuke　　　　　　　　　18
鰤大根・buri-daikon　鯛の兜煮・tai no kabuto-ni　　　　19
筑前煮・chikuzen-ni／がめ煮・game-ni　若竹煮・wakatake-ni　20
天ぷら・tempura　唐揚げ・kara-age　フライ・furai　　21
竹輪・chikuwa　蒲鉾・kamaboko　はんぺん・hampen　22
おから・okara／卯の花・unohana　白和え・shira-ae　　23
雁擬き・gammodoki／飛竜頭・hiryozu
味噌田楽・miso-dengaku　　　　　　　　　　　　　　　24
すき焼き・sukiyaki　しゃぶしゃぶ・shabu-shabu　　　　25
たこ焼き・takoyaki　お好み焼き・okonomiyaki　　　　　26
だし巻き玉子・dashimaki-tamago／玉子焼き・tamagoyaki
鰻の蒲焼・unagi no kabayaki　鰻の白焼・unagi no shirayaki　27
親子丼・oyako-donburi　木の葉丼・konoha-donburi　　　28
土瓶蒸し・dobin-mushi　茶碗蒸し・chawan-mushi　　　　29

麺類　Noodles

うどん・udon　そうめん・somen　　　　　　　　　　　30
きしめん・kishimen　中華めん・chukamen　　　　　　　31
蕎麦・soba　　　　　　　　　　　　　　　　　　　　32
せいろ蕎麦・seiro soba／ざる蕎麦・zaru soba
蕎麦猪口・soba-choko　薬味・yakumi　湯桶・yuto　　　33

きつね・kitsune／たぬき（大阪）・tanuki (in Osaka)
たぬき（関東）・tanuki (in Kanto)／
はいから（関西）・haikara (in Kansai)　　　　　　　　34
月見・tsukimi　山かけ・yamakake／とろろ・tororo　　35

寿司　Sushi

タネ・tane／ネタ・neta　しゃり・shari　　　　　　　36
ばらん・baran　手塩皿・teshio-zara／おてしょう・otesho
上がり・agari　　　　　　　　　　　　　　　　　　37
にぎり寿司・nigiri-zushi　　　　　　　　　　　　　38
軍艦巻き・gunkan-maki　細巻き・hoso-maki
玉子・tamago／玉・gyoku　がり・gari　　　　　　　39
鮪・maguro　　　　　　　　　　　　　　　　　　　40
鯛・tai　　　　　　　　　　　　　　　　　　　　　41
鰤・buri　　　　　　　　　　　　　　　　　　　　42
平目のえんがわ・hirame no engawa　　　　　　　　　43
鯵・aji　　　　　　　　　　　　　　　　　　　　　44
秋刀魚・samma　　　　　　　　　　　　　　　　　45
海老・ebi　　　　　　　　　　　　　　　　　　　　46
蝦蛄・shako　　　　　　　　　　　　　　　　　　　47
帆立・hotate　　　　　　　　　　　　　　　　　　　48
赤貝・akagai　　　　　　　　　　　　　　　　　　　49
烏賊・ika　　　　　　　　　　　　　　　　　　　　50
蛸・tako　　　　　　　　　　　　　　　　　　　　51
穴子・anago　　　　　　　　　　　　　　　　　　　52
てっさ・tessa　　　　　　　　　　　　　　　　　　53
イクラ軍艦巻き・ikura gunkan-maki
飛び子軍艦巻き・tobiko gunkan-maki　　　　　　　　54
ウニ軍艦巻き・uni gunkan-maki
蟹みそ軍艦巻き・kani-miso gunkan-maki　　　　　　　55
鉄火巻き・tekka-maki　かっぱ巻き・kappa-maki　　　56
太巻き・futo-maki　手巻き寿司・temaki-zushi　　　　57
稲荷寿司・inari-zushi　押し寿司・oshi-zushi　　　　　58
ちらし寿司（関東）・chirashi-zushi (in Kanto)
ちらし寿司（関西）・chirashi-zushi (in Kansai)　　　　59

ダシの材料　Ingredients of Soup Stock

鰹節・katsuobushi　昆布・kombu　　　　　　　　　60
鰯の煮干し・iwashi no niboshi　干し椎茸・hoshi-shiitake　61

香味野菜と香辛料　Herbs and Spices

つま・tsuma　けん・ken　辛み・karami　天盛り・temmori　63

吸口・suikuchi　椀種・wandane	
椀づま・wanzuma　吸地・suiji	65
山葵・wasabi　生姜・shoga　茗荷・myoga	66
木の芽・kinome　芽葱・menegi　防風・bofu	67
大葉・oba／青紫蘇・ao-jiso	
穂紫蘇・ho-jiso　花穂紫蘇・hanaho-jiso	68
青芽・aome　紫芽・murame	69
青柚子・ao-yuzu／青柚・aoyu	
かぼす・kabosu　すだち・sudachi	70
黄柚子・ki-yuzu　へぎ柚子・hegi-yuzu　刻み柚子・kizami-yuzu	
松葉柚子・matuba-yuzu	71

山菜　Edible Wild Plants

菜の花・nanohana／花菜・hanana　たらの芽・taranome	72
野蒜・nobiru　萱草・kanzo	73
山独活・yama-udo　土筆・tsukushi	74
蕨・warabi　薇・zemmai	75

和菓子　Confectionery

餡蜜・ammitsu　善哉・zenzai	76
羊羹・yokan　金鍔・kintsuba	77
薯蕷饅頭・joyo-manju　豆大福・mame-daifuku	78
今川焼き・imagawayaki／大判焼き・obanyaki／	
回転焼き・kaitenyaki	
どら焼き・dorayaki／三笠・mikasa　最中・monaka	79
金平糖・kompeito　有平糖・aruheito	80
落雁・rakugan　松風・matsukaze	81

季節の和菓子　Seasonal Confectionery

花びら餅・hanabira-mochi　鶯餅・uguisu-mochi	82
草餅・kusa-mochi／蓬餅・yomogi-mochi　桜餅・sakura-mochi	83
落とし文・otoshibumi　紫陽花金団・ajisai-kinton	84
葛饅頭・kuzu-manju　水（有平糖）・mizu (aruheito)	85
萩の餅・hagi no mochi／おはぎ・ohagi　吹き寄せ・fukiyose	86
亥の子餅・inoko-mochi／玄猪餅・gencho-mochi	
雪餅・yuki-mochi	87

茶　Tea

煎茶・sencha　玉露・gyokuro　抹茶・matcha	88
焙じ茶・hojicha　番茶・bancha	
玄米茶・gemmaicha　茎茶・kukicha／雁が音・karigane	89

酒　Alcoholic Drink

| 日本酒・nihonshu | 90 |
| 焼酎・shochu　泡盛・awamori | 91 |

食器
TABLEWARE

磁器　Porcelain

青磁・seiji　白磁・hakuji	94
染付・sometsuke　色絵・iroe	95
伊万里焼・imari-yaki／有田焼・arita-yaki	96
清水焼・kiyomizu-yaki　九谷焼・kutani-yaki	97

陶器　Ceramics

織部焼・oribe-yaki　志野焼・shino-yaki	98
信楽焼・shigaraki-yaki　伊賀焼・iga-yaki	99
常滑焼・tokoname-yaki	
備前焼・bizen-yaki／伊部焼・imbe-yaki	100
萩焼・hagi-yaki　唐津焼・karatsu-yaki	101

器　Tableware

四方皿・yoho-zara／角皿・kaku-zara	
長皿・naga-zara　俎板皿・manaita-zara	102
向付・mukozuke　なます皿・namasu-zara	103
手付鉢・tetsukibachi　片口・katakuchi	104
割山椒・warizansho　塗椀・nuriwan	105
八寸・hassun　曲げわっぱ・magewappa	
飯櫃・meshibitsu／おひつ・ohitsu	106
燗鍋・kan-nabe　朱杯・shuhai　杯台・haidai／sakazukidai	107
徳利・tokkuri (tokuri)／銚子・choshi	
徳利袴・tokkuri-bakama／銚子袴・choshi-bakama	108
猪口・choko／杯・sakazuki　ぐい呑み・guinomi	109

茶の道具　Tea Utensils

急須・kyusu　茶碗・chawan／湯呑み・yunomi	110
茶托・chataku／托子・takusu　茶筒・chazutsu	
茶匙・chasaji／茶箕・chami (chaki)　湯冷まし・yuzamashi	111

目次

7

抹茶の道具　Powdered Green Tea Utensils

抹茶茶碗・matcha-jawan　薄茶器・usuchaki／棗・natsume	112
茶筅・chasen　茶杓・chashaku	113

調理器具　Kitchen Utensils and Cookware

柳刃・yanagiba／正夫・shobu　出刃・deba　菜切・nakiri	114
擂り鉢と擂り粉木・suribachi and surikogi　胡麻煎り・gomairi	115
鬼おろし・oni-oroshi　鮫皮おろし・samekawa-oroshi	116
杓文字・shamoji　玉杓子・tamajakushi／おたま・otama	117
雪平鍋（行平鍋）・yukihira-nabe　落とし蓋・otoshibuta	118
卵焼き器・tamagoyaki-ki　親子鍋・oyako-nabe	119

箸　Chopsticks

柳箸・yanagi-bashi／祝い箸・iwai-bashi　盛箸・mori-bashi	120
利休箸・rikyu-bashi　黒文字・kuromoji	
青竹の箸・aotake no hashi	121

年中行事
ANNUAL EVENTS

正月（1月）　New Year (January)

門松・kadomatsu　鏡餅・kagami-mochi	124
注連飾り・shime-kazari	125
祝い肴三種・iwai-zakana sanshu／三つ肴・mitsu-zakana	
御節料理・osechi-ryori／祝い重・iwaiju	126
雑煮・zoni　屠蘇酒・tososhu	127

人日の節句（1月7日）　Festival of Seven Herbs (January 7th)

七草粥・nanakusagayu	128
せり・seri　なずな・nazuna　ごぎょう・gogyo	
はこべら・hakobera　ほとけのざ・hotokenoza	
すずな・suzuna　すずしろ・suzushiro	129

節分（2月3日頃）　Setsubun (Around February 3rd)

豆まき・mamemaki／追儺・tsuina／鬼やらい・oni-yarai	
恵方巻き・eho-maki	130
柊鰯・hiiragi-iwashi	131

8

上巳の節句／桃の節句／雛祭り（3月3日）
Girls' Doll Festival (March 3rd)

蛤のお吸い物・hamaguri no osuimono　菱餅・hishi-mochi	
ひなあられ・hina-arare	132
犬筥・inubako／御伽犬・otogi-inu　雪洞・bombori	133

端午の節句／こどもの日（5月5日）　Boy's Festival (May 5th)

鯉のぼり・koi-nobori	134
粽・chimaki　柏餅・kashiwa-mochi	135

夏越しの祓（6月30日）　Summer Passage Ritual (June 30th)

茅の輪くぐり・chinowa kuguri	136
水無月・minazuki	137

七夕（7月7日）　Tanabata Festival/Star Festival (July 7th)

笹飾り・sasa-kazari	138
素麺・somen	
願いの糸・negai no ito／五色の麻苧・goshiki no asao	139

お盆／盂蘭盆会（旧暦7月15日前後）
Bon Festival/Lantern Festival (Middle of July on the Lunar Calendar)

迎え火・mukaebi	140
精霊馬・shoryo-uma　精進料理・shojin-ryori	141

十五夜の月見・中秋の名月・芋名月（旧暦8月15日）
Moon-viewing (August 15th on the Lunar Calendar)

月見飾り・tsukimi-kazari	143

重陽の節句（9月9日）　Chrysanthemum Festival (September 9th)

茱萸袋・gumi-bukuro　菊の被綿・kiku no kisewata	144
菊酒・kiku-zake　栗ご飯・kuri-gohan	145

大晦日／大つごもり（12月31日）　New Year's Eve

年越し蕎麦・toshikoshi-soba／つごもり蕎麦・tsugomori-soba	146
おけら詣り・okera-mairi	147

和食の調味料　Seasonings for Washoku	92
嫌い箸　Chopstick Taboos	122

索引（五十音順）　Index for Japanese	148

本書の英訳について

1. モノ・コトの名前には、読み方（ヘボン式ローマ字表記）と英語名を掲載しています。英語名は基本的に『日本語から引く「食」ことば英語辞典』（服部幸應監修・小学館）に準拠していますが、必ずしも定型表現ではありません。
2. 日本語の説明文と、英語の説明文とが対応していない場合（英訳では解説を割愛した箇所）があります。
3. 英訳文の中で、日本語読みのまま使用していることばは、イタリック（斜体）表記にしていますが、Oxford Advanced Learner's Dictionary 8th edition に英語として登録されていることばは正体にしています。
4. 料理の説明文中に出てくる調味料については、92頁で紹介しています。

About the Translation

1. The pronunciation of Japanese words in this book is written in the Hepburn Romanization system. As for the English translations, we have referred to *Nihongo kara hiku shoku kotoba eigojiten* (Japanese-English Dictionary of Food and Cooking). However, please note that the English names may not necessarily be a fixed translation.
2. In some parts, explanations have been omitted in the course of translating from Japanese to English.
3. Japanese words are shown in italic, except those in the Oxford Advanced Learner's Dictionary 8th Edition, which are in normal font.
4. Japanese seasonings in the cooking pages are introduced on page 92.

和食

JAPANESE COOKING

会席料理

和食のコース料理を「会席」「懐石」という。「懐石」という字は本来、茶会の料理を指すが、近年は混用されている。献立（品書き）の名前や順番は、店によって異なる。

先付・*sakizuke* ／ 付出し・*tsukidashi*
First Dish in the Course

前菜として、あるいは前菜の前に出される最初の一品。

The first dish served in a course as an appetizer, or before an appetizer. Similar to the amuse-bouche in French cuisine.

椀盛・*wanmori* ／ 椀物・*wanmono*
Clear Soup of the Season

旬の食材を取り合わせた具に澄まし汁をはって、塗椀（105頁）に盛り付けた料理。

A dish served in a lacquerware soup bowl (page 105), with seasonal ingredients in clear soup (lightly seasoned soup stock).

Course Dishes (*kaiseki-ryori*)

The names given to each type of dish and the order in which they are served depend on each restaurant.

向付・*mukozuke*
造り・*tsukuri*
刺身・*sashimi*
Sashimi

新鮮な魚介を薄く切った料理。香味野菜と香辛料（62頁）を添え、醤油などをつけて食べる。

Thinly sliced fresh seafood such as fish or shellfish. Served with herbs and spices (page 62) and eaten with soy sauce.

焼物・*yakimono*
Broiled Dish

魚介や肉などを焼いた料理。会席のメイン料理の一つ。

Grilled fish or meat. One of the main dishes for *kaiseki*.

煮物・*nimono* ／炊き合せ・*takiawase*
Assorted Simmered Dish

魚介類・野菜などを一つ一つ煮て、器に盛り合わせた料理。
Simmered fish, shellfish and vegetables, served together in a bowl.

揚物・*agemono*
Deep-fried Dish

食材を油で揚げた料理。会席では素揚げ、天ぷら、唐揚げ（21頁）が多い。

Mostly *suage* (fried without batter), tempura (dipped in flour-based batter before frying; page 21) or *kara-age* (coated with flour or starch before frying; page 21).

強肴・*shiizakana*／進肴・*susumezakana*
Side Dish

お酒を勧めるために出される一品。酢の物や珍味など、料理は多様。

Various dishes are served, such as vinegared dishes or delicacies.

ご飯・*gohan*
Rice

白米もしくは季節の炊き込みご飯。会席では最後に出される。

White rice, or steamed rice with seasonal ingredients. Served as the last dish in *kaiseki*.

止椀・*tomewan*
Miso Soup

ご飯とともに出される味噌汁。季節によって赤味噌、白味噌、合わせ味噌が使い分けられる。

Served together with rice. Different types of miso are used according to the seasons, such as red, white or blended miso.

香の物・*konomono*
Pickled Vegetables

野菜の漬物のこと。塩漬け、糠漬けなどの種類がある。

There are various types such as vegetables pickled in salt or in salted rice-bran paste.

1

2

1
水菓子・*mizugashi*
Fruits

コースの最後を締めくくる季節の果物。
Fruits of the season, to wrap up the course.

2
甘味・*kammi*
Sweets

甘いもの。和菓子が多く、抹茶が出されることもある。
Mostly *wagashi* (Japanese confectionary). *Matcha*, powdered green tea, may be served with it.

定番料理

家庭でも親しまれている、和食の定番料理や食品を紹介。

鯖の味噌煮・*saba no miso-ni*
Mackerel Simmered in Miso Sauce

鯖の切り身を、ダシと味噌で煮た料理。生姜の薄切りを加えて煮込むと青魚特有の生臭さが抑えられる。

Slices of mackerel simmered in broth and miso. By cooking with thinly sliced ginger, the fishy smell particular to blue-backed fish can be reduced.

金目鯛の煮付け・*kimmedai no nitsuke*
Simmered Alfonsino

金目鯛を酒、みりん、醤油でさっと煮た料理。金目鯛は、目が大きく金色に光るためにこの名が付いているが、タイの仲間ではない。

Alfonsino simmered in sake, *mirin* and soy sauce. In Japanese, "*kimmedai*" means sea bream (*tai/dai*) with gold eyes (*kimme*). However, it is not a kind of sea bream.

Classic Dishes

Classic *washoku* dishes and ingredients that are also enjoyed in the home.

鰤大根・*buri-daikon*
Yellowtail Simmered with Daikon Radish

冬が旬の鰤（ぶり）と大根を一緒に煮た料理。鰤の旨味を大根が吸っておいしくなる。

Yellowtail is best in winter. The daikon radish absorbs the umami of the yellowtail, making the dish very tasty.

鯛の兜煮・*tai no kabuto-ni*
Simmered Head of Sea Bream

鯛の頭を煮付けた料理。その姿を武士がかぶった兜に見立てて「兜煮」と呼ばれる。鯛は「めでたい」の語呂合わせから、祝い事に欠かせない食材。

The head of the sea bream is likened to a samurai's helmet (*kabuto*), which gave the dish its Japanese name *kabuto-ni*. In Japanese, there is an adjective pronounced *medetai* used to indicate something happy. Since this word rhymes with *tai*, meaning "sea bream," this fish is essential for celebrations.

筑前煮・*chikuzen-ni* ／ がめ煮・*game-ni*
Chikuzen-style Stew

鶏肉と、人参・牛蒡（ごぼう）・蓮根（れんこん）といった根菜類を炒めてから煮た料理。本来は、筑前地方（福岡県）の郷土料理だった。

Chicken stir-fried and simmered with root crops such as carrots, burdocks and lotus roots. Originally a local specialty of the area called Chikuzen which is today's Fukuoka Prefecture.

若竹煮・*wakatake-ni*
Simmered Bamboo Shoots with *Wakame*

春が旬の竹の子（筍）と若布（わかめ）を炊き合わせた料理。木の芽（67頁）と呼ばれる山椒の新芽を添える。

Bamboo shoots (best in spring) and *wakame* (seaweed) are simmered separately then served together, garnished with Japanese pepper leaves which are called *kinome* (page 67).

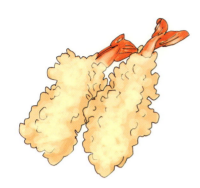

天ぷら・*tempura*
Tempura

水溶きした小麦粉と溶き卵を合わせた衣に、食材をつけて揚げる料理法。語源は諸説あり、ポルトガル語で調味料を意味するtemperoから来たとされる。

A way of cooking where ingredients are dipped in batter made from water, flour and egg, then deep-fried. As for the etymology of tempura, although other theories exist, one is that it comes from "tempero," which is Portuguese word meaning "seasoning."

唐揚げ・*kara-age*
Deep-fried Food

食材に片栗粉もしくは小麦粉をつけて揚げる料理法。鶏肉を用いる「鶏の唐揚げ」が最も好まれる。粉をつけない揚げ方は「素揚げ」という。

A way of cooking in which ingredients are coated with starch or flour before frying. The most popular dish is fried chicken. When ingredients are fried without flour or starch, they are referred to as *suage*.

フライ・*furai*
Deep-fried Food with Bread Crumbs

食材に小麦粉、溶き卵、パン粉の順で衣をつけ、揚げる料理法。西洋料理を真似て日本で創作された。ちなみに、英語のfryは少量の油で炒めたり揚げたりする料理法をいう。

A way of Western-influenced cooking invented in Japan, where ingredients are coated in flour, dipped in beaten eggs, sprinkled with bread crumbs then deep-fried.

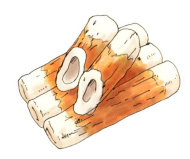

竹輪・*chikuwa*

Cylindrical Fish Sausage

魚の身をすりつぶして練ったものを、細い竹串や金属の串に塗りつけて、焼いたり蒸したりする食品。竹串を抜くと輪状になることからの名前。

Ground and kneaded fish paste wrapped around thin bamboo sticks or metal sticks, then grilled or steamed. The two kanji characters used in this name mean "bamboo shoot" and "ring," expressing the appearance of this food.

蒲鉾・*kamaboko*

Steamed Fish Paste Cake

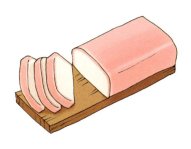

魚の身をすりつぶして練り、板に盛って蒸した食品。かつては現在の「竹輪」と同じ筒状で、蒲（がま）の穂や、長い柄の先に刃物をつけた鉾（ほこ）に似ていたことからのネーミングとされる。

Ground and kneaded fish paste heaped on a board and steamed. Before, it was also tube-shaped like today's *chikuwa* and it is said that the name was given due to its appearance which looked like the head of a cattail (*kama*) or like a pike (*hoko*).

はんぺん・*hampen*

Fish-cake Made of Fish Paste and Yam

魚のすり身に卵白や山芋を混ぜて蒸した、やわらかい食品。語源には駿河国（静岡県）の料理人・半平（はんぺい）が創作したなど諸説ある。

Made by steaming grounded fish mixed with egg white and grated yam. Several different etymologies exist, one being that a cook in Suruga (today's Shizuoka Prefecture) named Hanbei made this.

おから・*okara* ／卯の花・*unohana*
Dish with Tofu Refuse

豆腐をつくる過程でできる豆乳の絞りかすを「おから」もしくは「卯の花」といい、これを使った料理も「おから」「卯の花」と呼んでいる。語源には諸説あるが、絞り殻（から）に御を付けて「おから」、ウツギの白い花（別名・卯の花）にたとえて「卯の花」という説などが一般的。

Okara or *unohana* refers to the residue of soy milk that is produced in the process of making tofu. Dishes that use these two are also called *okara* or *unohana*. Among several different etymologies, the most general ones are that *okara* is a polite way of saying *kara*, which indicates the residue, and that *unohana* comes from the white flowers of deutzias, known as *unohana* in Japanese.

白和え・*shira-ae*
Tofu Dressing

豆腐をすり、白胡麻などと合わせた衣で、野菜の細切りを和えた料理。黒胡麻を合わせたものは「黒和え」という。

Thinly sliced vegetables dressed with mashed tofu mixed with white sesame seeds. "*Shira*" means "white" in Japanese, therefore the dish is called *kuro-ae* ("*kuro*" means "black") when black sesame seeds are used.

雁擬き・*gammodoki*／飛竜頭・*hiryozu*
Deep-fried Tofu Burger

崩した豆腐にすりおろした山芋を混ぜ、細かく刻んだ野菜などを加えて揚げた食品。「雁擬き」は、渡り鳥のガンに似ているという意味のネーミング。「飛竜頭」は、ポルトガルの揚げ菓子filhosにちなむという。

Made by first mashing tofu, mixing it together with ground yam and vegetables chopped in small pieces, then deep-frying the mix. "*Ganmodoki*" means "looks like wild geese." *Hiryozu* is said to derive from a Portuguese fried dessert, "*filhos*."

味噌田楽・*miso-dengaku*
Grilled Food Coated with Miso Glaze

豆腐を短冊形に切って竹串に刺し、調味した味噌を塗って焼く料理。こんにゃくや野菜も用いられる。田楽とは、田植えのときに豊作を祈って奉納する踊りで、串に刺した姿が田楽を踊る人に似ていることから付いた名前といわれる。

Tofu cut in rectangles, fixed on skewers, brushed with seasoned miso then grilled. *Konnyaku* and vegetables are also used. *Dengaku* is a dance performed in rice-planting ceremonies, to wish for an abundant harvest. It is said that tofu fixed on skewers look like the dancers of *dengaku*, which gave this dish its name.

すき焼き・*sukiyaki*
Sukiyaki

薄切り牛肉と野菜類を焼きながら食べる鍋料理。関西では、醤油と砂糖などの調味料を別々に加えて味付けする。関東では、ダシに調味料を加えた「割下（わりした）」を用いる。溶き卵につけて食べるのが一般的。

A type of hot pot with thin beef slices and vegetables. In the Kansai region, seasonings such as soy sauce and sugar are added separately, while in the Kanto region, a sauce made from broth and seasonings are used. Before eating, the fried ingredients are dipped in raw egg.

しゃぶしゃぶ・*shabu-shabu*
shabu-shabu

ダシを煮立て、薄切り牛肉をさっとくぐらせて、ポン酢やゴマダレにつけて食べる鍋料理。野菜、豆腐なども加える。語源は、肉を「しゃぶしゃぶ」とダシの中で泳がすことから。

A type of hot pot where thin beef is blanched in broth and eaten with *ponzu* sauce or sesame sauce. Other ingredients such as vegetables and tofu are also eaten together. "*Shabu-shabu*" is an onomatopoeia for the sound made when moving the meat in the broth as if washing something in water, which gave the dish its name.

たこ焼き・*takoyaki*

Small Ball of Wheat Flour with Bits of Octopus

水で溶いた小麦粉の生地に蛸の切り身を入れ、専用の鉄板で球状に丸めながら焼いた関西の人気料理。ソースと鰹節（60頁）や青海苔をかける。

A popular dish in the Kansai region, made by grilling balls of flour-based batter with pieces of octopus in the middle. A special iron plate is used to grill them in ball shapes. Enjoyed with sauce, dried bonito shavings (page 60) and dried green seaweed.

お好み焼き・*okonomiyaki*

Japanese Pancake Fried with Various Ingredients

水で溶いた小麦粉の生地に魚介類・肉・野菜など好みの具材を混ぜ合わせ、鉄板で円形に焼いた関西の人気料理。広島では中華めんといっしょに焼くなど、地方色がある。

A popular dish in the Kansai region. Ingredients such as fish, shellfish, meat or vegetables are mixed in flour-based batter, then grilled in round shapes on an iron plate. Each area has its own way of making this dish. For example, in Hiroshima Prefecture, Chinese noodles are fried with the mixture.

だし巻き玉子・*dashimaki-tamago*
玉子焼き・*tamagoyaki*
Omelet

溶き卵にダシを混ぜて、卵焼き器(119頁)を用いて巻き重ねながら焼いた料理。ダシを使わず、調味料で好みの味をつけて焼いたものは「玉子焼き」という。

Beaten eggs mixed with broth are fried and rolled up in thin layers using a special pan (*tamagoyaki-ki*; page 119). When other seasonings are used in place of broth, it is referred to as *tamagoyaki* and not *dashimaki-tamago*, since "*dashi*" means "broth."

鰻の蒲焼・*unagi no kabayaki*
鰻の白焼・*unagi no shirayaki*
Broiled Eel Flavored with Thick Sweetened Soy Sauce /
Broiled Eel without Sauce

「鰻の蒲焼」は鰻を開いて数本の串に刺し、醤油ベースの甘ダレをつけながら焼いた料理。関西では、鰻を蒸してから焼くことが多い。「鰻の白焼」はタレをつけずに焼いたもので、醤油をつけながら食べる。「蒲焼」といえば鰻のそれを指すが、語源には諸説ある。

Unagi no kabayaki is eel (*unagi*), skewered and dipped in sweet soy sauce-based sauce before broiling. In the Kansai region, it is common to steam the eel before broiling. *Unagi no shirayaki* is broiled without the sauce, and is eaten with soy sauce. The term *kabayaki* refers to that of *unagi*, but there are a number of etymologies.

親子丼・*oyako-domburi*

Bowl of Rice Topped with Chicken and Egg

鶏肉をダシで煮て卵でとじ、どんぶりに盛ったご飯の上にそれをかけた料理。鶏と卵を、親と子どもに見立てた名前で、豚肉を用いた場合は「他人丼」という。

Bowl of rice topped with chicken and egg simmered in broth. "*Oyako*" means "parent and child" in Japanese, referring to the chicken and egg used in this dish. When pork is used instead of chicken, it is called *tanin-donburi*. "*Tanin*" means "stranger."

木の葉丼・*konoha-domburi*

Bowl of Rice Topped with *Kamaboko*, Vegetables and Egg

薄切りの蒲鉾（かまぼこ・22頁）とネギなどの野菜を煮て卵でとじ、どんぶりに盛ったご飯の上にそれをかけた料理。関西発祥の料理で、蒲鉾を舞い散る木の葉に見立てたネーミング。

Bowl of rice topped with simmered thinly sliced *kamaboko* (page 22) and vegetables such as long green onions, finished with egg. Originally from the Kansai region. The *kamaboko* used in this dish are likened to leaves, which gave this dish its name.

土瓶蒸し・*dobin-mushi*
Food Cooked in an Earthen Teapot

松茸と鱧（はも）などと澄まし汁を土瓶に入れ、土瓶ごと蒸す、秋の高級料理。土瓶とセットの猪口に汁を注ぎ、すだち（70頁）を絞って飲む。

Ingredients such as *matsutake* mushrooms and conger pike eel, put together in an earthen teapot (*dobin*), and steamed in clear soup. An autumn haute cuisine. The soup is poured in a small cup that comes with the teapot, and *sudachi* (page 70) juice is squeezed over it before drinking.

茶碗蒸し・*chawan-mushi*
Egg Custard Steamed in a Cup

魚介類や鶏肉、三つ葉などの具材と、卵を加えたダシを小さな茶碗に入れて蒸した料理。関西の料理店の定番メニューだが、発祥は長崎県とされる。

Ingredients such as fish, shellfish, chicken and *mitsuba* are mixed with broth and egg, and put in a small cup (*chawan*) to steam. While it is a classic dish in restaurants in the Kansai region, it is said to have been first made in Nagasaki Prefecture.

麺類

日本には、原材料や形の異なるさまざまな麺がある。ここでは代表的なものを紹介する。

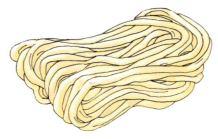

うどん・*udon*
Udon Noodles

小麦粉に水と塩を加えてこね、延ばして線状に切った麺。温かいつゆに入れ、肉や野菜、卵や天ぷらを加えて食べるのが一般的。夏には冷たいうどんメニューもある。

Made by kneading wheat flour with water and salt, then rolling out the dough and cutting it to form noodles. Generally eaten with meat, vegetables, eggs or tempura in hot noodle soup. Eaten cold in summer.

そうめん・*somen*
Fine Wheat Noodles

小麦粉に水、塩を加えてこねた生地に油を塗ってから、細く引き延ばして乾燥させた白く細い麺。主に夏に食べられる。そうめんより少し太い麺を「冷や麦」というが、そうめんとは製法が異なる。

Wheat flour is kneaded with water and salt to make the dough, which is then coated with oil before being rolled up and dried. Mainly eaten in summer. Noodles that are slightly thicker than *somen* are called *hiyamugi*, and are produced in a different way.

Noodles

In Japan, there are various types of noodles made from different ingredients and in different shapes. Here are some of the more common noodles.

きしめん・*kishimen*
Flat Wheat Noodles

平打ちにしたうどんを、名古屋では「きしめん」という。語源は諸説あり、竹筒を使って棊子（きし・碁石のこと）の形に抜いてつくったのが原型という説もある。群馬県では「ひもかわ」と呼ばれている。

Flat *udon* is called *kishimen* in Nagoya. In Gunma Prefecture, this type of noodle is called *himokawa*.

中華めん・*chukamen*
Chinese Noodles

小麦粉を、かんすい（食品添加物として認められている炭酸ナトリウム、炭酸カリウムなどのアルカリ性物質）を加えた水でこねてつくる麺。ラーメン、中華そば、焼きそばなどに用いられる。

Wheat flour is kneaded with lye water (an alkaline substance authorized as an additive, such as sodium carbonate or potassium carbonate) to make this yellow noodle. Used for dishes such as *ramen* noodles and *yakisoba* (fried noodles).

1
蕎麦・*soba*
Soba Noodles

ソバの実を挽いた粉に水と小麦粉などのつなぎを加えてこねて延ばし、線状に切った麺。蕎麦殻を取り除いてから挽いた蕎麦と、殻ごと挽いた蕎麦で、色が異なる。

Buckwheat flour kneaded with water and binders such as wheat flour, rolled out and cut to form noodles. The color of *soba* depends on whether the hulls had been removed or not before grinding the buckwheat.

2

せいろ蕎麦・*seiro soba*
ざる蕎麦・*zaru soba*

Cold *Soba* Noodles Served in a *Seiro* or a *Zaru*

熱湯で茹で上げ冷水でしめた蕎麦メニューを「せいろ」もしくは「ざる」という。江戸時代に蒸籠（せいろ）で蒸していたなごりで「せいろ」に盛り付けたり、茹でる際に用いる「ざる」に盛ったりすることからの名前。

Soba noodles that are boiled and served cold are called *seiro* or *zaru*. They are served in a *seiro* (a steamer) which was used for steaming the noodles in the 17th century, or in a *zaru* (a draining basket) which is used for cooking the noodles in hot water.

3

蕎麦猪口・*soba-choko*

Dipping Soup Cup for *Soba*

蕎麦を浸すためのつゆを入れる、小さな器。猪口（109頁）は本来、酒を飲むときの器をいう。

Soba noodles are dipped in this soup before enjoying them. *Choko* (page 109) is originally a term used to indicate cups for drinking sake.

4

薬味・*yakumi*

Condiment

料理に添えて、風味や食欲を増したりする香味野菜と香辛料。冷たい蕎麦には葱と山葵（わさび・66頁）が一般的。

Herbs and spices that are used as condiments to add flavor and to work up an appetite. For cold *soba*, long green onions and wasabi (page 66) are common.

5

湯桶・*yuto*

Sobayu Pot

蕎麦の茹で汁「蕎麦湯」を入れる漆塗りの器。蕎麦を食べたあと、残ったつゆに蕎麦湯を加えて飲む。

A lacquerware pot for serving *sobayu*, the hot water (*yu*) which was used to boil the noodles. After eating *soba*, *sobayu* is added to the leftover noodle soup to drink.

きつね・*kitsune*
たぬき（大阪）・*tanuki (in Osaka)*
Soba or *Udon* with *Abura-age*

甘辛く煮た油揚げがのった蕎麦・うどんを「きつね」という。大阪では、油揚げがのったうどんを「きつね」、蕎麦は「たぬき」と区別する。「きつね」は油揚げを意味し、狐（きつね）の好物とされていたことに由来する。

Soba or *udon* topped with salty-sweet simmered *abura-age* (thin deep-fried tofu) is called *kitsune* (fox). In Osaka, *udon* with *abura-age* is called *kitsune* and *soba* with *abura-age* is called *tanuki* (racoon dog). *Kitsune* indicates *abura-age*, because in popular myth, *abura-age* is said to be a favorite of foxes.

たぬき（関東）・*tanuki (in Kanto)*
はいから（関西）・*haikara (in Kansai)*
Soba or *Udon* with *Tenkasu*

天ぷらを揚げたときにできる天かす（揚げ玉）がのった蕎麦・うどんを関東では「たぬき」といい、大阪・京都では「はいから」という。また、京都の「たぬき」は、きつねうどんのダシをあんかけにしたものになる。

Soba or *udon* with *tenkasu* (bits of deep-fried tempura batter) is called *tanuki* in Kanto and *haikara* in Osaka and Kyoto. *Tanuki* in Kyoto refers to an *ankake* (thick, starchy soup) *udon* noodles with *abura-age*.

月見・*tsukimi*

Soba or *Udon* Topped with a Raw Egg

生卵が入った蕎麦・うどん。「月見（月を見る）」の文字通り、卵の黄身を月に見立てたネーミング。

As the name suggests with the kanji characters for "moon" and "see," the yolk is likened to the moon.

山かけ・*yamakake* / とろろ・*tororo*

Soba or *Udon* Topped with Grated Yam

山芋や長芋のすりおろしをのせた蕎麦・うどん。「山かけ」は「山芋掛け」の略称。「とろろ」は、トロっとした粘りのある食感から付いた名前。山芋や長芋のことも「とろろ芋」と呼ぶ。

Soba or *udon* with grated yam or Chinese yam. The name *tororo* comes from a Japanese onomatopoeia "*torotoro*" which expresses stickiness. Yam and Chinese yam are also called *tororo-imo* (*tororo* yam).

寿司

古くは魚を保存するためにご飯で自然発酵させたものを「酸し」といった。今では新鮮な魚をのせたにぎり寿司が代名詞になっている。

1
タネ・*tane* / ネタ・*neta*　　Ingredients of Sushi

寿司にのせる魚介などの材料＝寿司種のこと。ネタはタネの逆読みで、業界内で使われる言葉（隠語）だったが、現在は一般化している。

The ingredients of sushi, such as fish or shellfish. When *tane* is read backwards, it becomes *neta*.

2
しゃり・*shari*　　White Rice

白いご飯のこと。特に寿司飯に使う。寿司飯は酢を加えた白飯が一般的。大切な米粒を釈迦の遺骨「仏舎利（ぶっしゃり）」にたとえたネーミング。

This term is used especially when referring to sushi rice. For sushi, it is common to use vinegared white rice. Rice, which is an important food for the Japanese, has been likened to the remains of Buddha (*busshari*) which is why it is called *shari*.

Sushi

In the old times, sushi (with the kanji for "acid") referred to fish that had been naturally fermented for preservation, by using cooked rice. Today, sushi has become synonymous with *nigiri-zushi*, oblong fingers of vinegared rice topped with slices of fresh raw fish.

3

ばらん・*baran*

Partition Sheet

寿司や弁当に用いられる仕切り。香りや味が移らないように、料理と料理の間に置く。現在はプラスチック製が主流。本来はハランの葉でつくられたため、「ハラン」が語源とされている。

Partition sheets for sushi or *bento*. These are used to separate food so that the smell and taste of food will not mix with one another. Today, ones made from plastic are common. They were traditionally made from the leaves of *haran*, or aspidistra in English, which is the origin for the name *baran*.

4

手塩皿・*teshio-zara* ／ おてしよう・*otesho*

Small Plate for Soy Sauce

醬油を入れる小さくて浅い皿のこと。本来、食膳の不浄を払うために置いた、塩を盛った皿のことをいう。

A small shallow plate used for serving soy sauce. Originally refers to a plate with a pile of salt, which was placed in order to purify the table.

5

上がり・*agari*

Green Tea

お茶のこと。淹れたてのお茶を意味する「上がり花」の略。昔、遊郭で使われていた言葉で、「上がり」はお茶、「花」は端(はな)＝最初を意味する。客がつかず暇をもてあましていることを「お茶を挽く」というため、「お茶」を嫌い、客が登楼する意味の「上がり」と言い換えたともいわれる。

Short for the term *agarihana*, which means tea that has just been made. "*Agari*" means "tea" and "*hana*" (with the kanji for "flower") means "first." This term was once used in the *yukaku* (red-light districts).

1
にぎり寿司・*nigiri-zushi*
Hand-shaped Sushi

酢飯を片手で握って俵状にし、その上にタネ（36頁）をのせたもの。「にぎり飯」というと、通常はご飯を両手の大きさに握った「おにぎり」や「おむすび」のことを指す。

Vinegared rice shaped into oblong, topped with *tane* (page 36). *Nigirimeshi* normally refers to hand-sized rice balls which are called *onigiri* or *omusubi*. *Zushi* is the same as sushi, although the pronunciation has been modified.

2

軍艦巻き・*gunkan-maki*
Battleship Roll

握った酢飯を海苔で巻き、その上に形がくずれやすいタネをのせた寿司の一種。横から見た姿が軍艦に似ていることからのネーミング。

Shaped vinegared rice wrapped with *nori* (a sheet of dried seaweed) and topped with *tane* that cannot keep shape. This sushi resembles battleships when looked at from the side, which gave its name, *gunkan-maki* (battleship roll).

3

細巻き・*hoso-maki*
Thin Roll

巻き簾(まきす・調理用のすだれ)の上に海苔をひろげて酢飯をのせ、タネを芯にして巻いた寿司の一種。

A type of sushi which is made by spreading *nori* and vinegared rice on a *makisu* (bamboo mat), putting *tane* on it, then rolling it.

4

玉子・*tamago*／玉・*gyoku*
Omelet

玉子焼き(27頁)のこと。寿司店で供される玉子焼きは、海老や白身魚のすり身と卵を混ぜ合わせて焼いたもの。

Same as *tamago-yaki* (page 27). *Tamago* served in sushi restaurants have ground prawn or white fish paste mixed in with the egg.

5

がり・*gari*
Pickled Ginger

口直しのための、甘酢漬けの生姜。語源は、大きな生姜をかつては丸のままガリっとかじったことから。

Thinly-sliced ginger pickled in sweetened vinegar, for cleansing the palate. The name comes from the onomatopoeia "*gari*" which expresses the sound made when biting into a large piece of ginger.

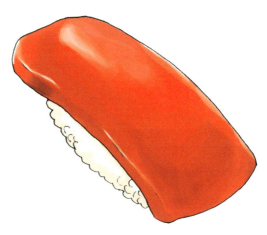

鮪・*maguro*
Tuna

最も代表的な寿司種の一つ。部位によって名称が異なり、赤身(中心部)、大トロ(腹の上部)、中トロ(腹の中部と下部、背)などがある。

One of the most popular ingredients of sushi. Each part of *maguro* (tuna) has a different name. For example, *akami* (lean meat), *otoro* (fatty tuna) and *chutoro* (medium fatty tuna).

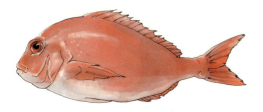

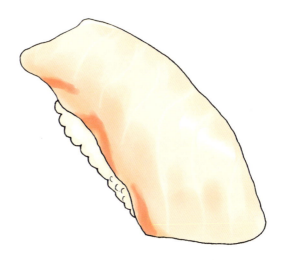

鯛・*tai*
Sea Bream

近海で獲れる白身魚で、天然ものと養殖ものがある。日本の祝い事に欠かせない魚で、さまざまな料理に使われる。頭は、鯛の兜煮（19頁）などにする。

A type of whitefish in the coastal waters of Japan. There are both wild and farmed sea breams. Essential for celebratory occasions, and used in various dishes. Simmered Head of Sea Bream (page 19) is one representative dish.

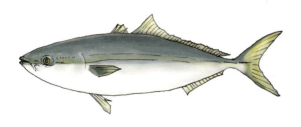

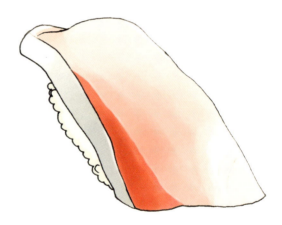

鰤・*buri*
Yellowtail

脂がのった魚で、成長するに従い名前が変わる。地方によって異なるが、関東ではイナダ→ワラサ→ブリ、関西ではハマチ→メジロ→ブリと呼ばれることが多い。料理では鰤大根（19頁）が有名。

The Japanese amberjack changes its name as it grows. Although this varies according to each region, in Kanto, it goes from *inada* to *warasa* to *buri*, whereas in Kansai it goes from *hamachi* to *mejiro* to *buri*. One popular dish is Yellowtail Simmered with Daikon Radish (page 19).

平目のえんがわ・*hirame no engawa*
Fluke Fin of Olive Flounder

えんがわとは「縁側」の意味で、背びれや腹びれの付け根にある活動筋をいう。コリコリした食感で脂がのっているので好まれる。上品な白身の平目は、ポン酢で食べることが多い。

Engawa is the flesh at the base of the dorsal and ventral fins. This word is also used for Japanese-style narrow wooden passageways. The white olive flounder is often eaten with *ponzu* sauce.

鯵 · *aji*

Horse Mackerel

日本各地の近海で獲れる小魚。味が良いので「味（あじ）」と呼んだとされる。鯵（あじ）や鯖（さば）、秋刀魚（さんま）など、体の表面が青光りする魚の類を「青魚」「青背の魚」「光り物（ひかりもの）」と呼ぶ。

A small fish caught in many coastal areas of Japan. It is said to have been named *aji* due to its good taste, or good *aji* in Japanese. Horse mackerel and other fish that shine blue such as mackerel or saury, are all referred to as "bluefish."

Sushi

秋刀魚・*samma*
Saury

日本の秋の風物詩でもある魚。文字通り、日本刀のような姿をしている。臭みを消すために、アサツキや生姜を添えることがある。

Saury is an autumnal fish. As the kanji characters used for this fish so indicate—"autumn," "sword" and "fish,"—it resembles a Japanese sword. Chives or ginger may be eaten with saury to get rid of the fishy smell.

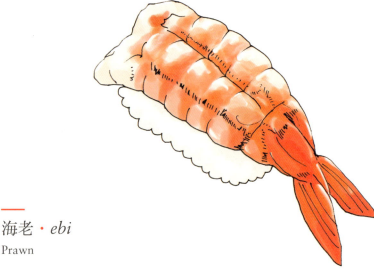

海老・*ebi*
Prawn

日本は世界一の海老消費国であり、昔から人気の寿司種。蒸した海老から生で食べる車海老、牡丹海老、甘海老まで種類は多い。長いひげを持ち、腰の曲がった姿が老人に似ていることから、長寿を象徴する縁起物でもある。

Japan is the largest *ebi*-consuming country in the world. *Ebi* is a long-time popular ingredient of sushi that can be eaten either steamed or raw. Various kinds exist such as prawns, peony shrimp and sweet shrimp. *Ebi* symbolize longevity due to their long mustaches and bent backs, which resemble that of an old man.

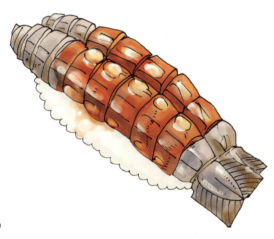

蝦蛄・*shako*
Squilla

海老に似た甲殻類。関東や瀬戸内地方で好まれる。生の蝦蛄は灰色だが、茹でるとシャクナゲの花に似た色になることからのネーミング。

A crustacean which looks similar to an *ebi* (prawn). Eaten in the Kanto and Setouchi regions.

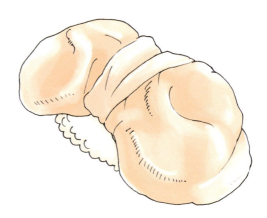

帆立・*hotate*
Scallop

帆立貝の、大きく発達した貝柱の部分を寿司種にする。帆立貝の語源は諸説あるが、殻を激しく開閉して泳ぐ様子が、帆を立てて移動する船に似ていることからという。

The large adductor muscle of a scallop is eaten as sushi.

赤貝・*akagai*
Ark Shell

身が朱色であるのが特徴的な貝の一種。貝殻には隆起した筋が、放射線状に42本前後ある。ヒモと呼ばれる部分は、胡瓜と一緒に海苔で巻いて「ひもきゅう」にすることもある。

Ark shells have red flesh. The shells have around 42 lines that radiate from the center. The exterior mantle, called *himo*, can be eaten with cucumber by wrapping them together in *nori* (a sheet of seaweed). This dish is called *himokyu*.

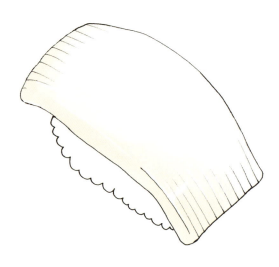

烏賊・*ika*
Squid

烏賊にもいろいろな種類があるが、寿司種としてはスルメイカ、アオリイカ、ヤリイカが一般的。語源は、姿が「いかめしい（厳しい）」ことからなど諸説ある。

Although many different kinds exist, popular ones used for sushi are cuttlefish, oval squid and spear squid.

蛸・*tako*

Octopus

烏賊と同様、いろいろな種類があるが、寿司種としてはマダコ、北海タコが一般的。日本では寿司種以外にもさまざまな料理に使われ、庶民的な料理ではたこ焼き（26頁）が有名。

Popular varieties used for sushi are *madako* (common octopus) and *hokkai tako* (North Pacific giant octopus), among others. In addition to sushi, they are used in a variety of dishes such as *takoyaki* (page 26), which is a very common dish in Japan.

穴子・*anago*
Conger Eel

穴子はウナギの仲間で、砂地などの狭い穴に住んでいるところからの名前という。寿司では、醬油やみりんで煮た穴子に、煮汁を煮詰めた「詰め」を塗る。

The Japanese name is *anago* with the kanji characters for "hole" and "child" because they live in narrow holes in sandy soil. For sushi, they are simmered with soy sauce and *mirin*.

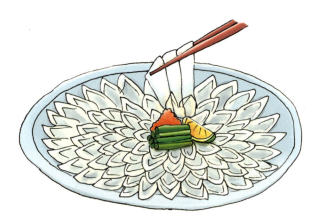

てっさ・*tessa*

Sashimi of Globefish

河豚（ふぐ）の刺身。関西では、猛毒を持った河豚を、当たると死ぬ鉄砲にたとえ、刺身を「鉄刺（てっさ）」、皮を「鉄皮（てっぴ）」、河豚鍋を「鉄ちり（てっちり）」と呼んでいる。関西の寿司店には河豚が欠かせない。

Sashimi of *fugu*, or globefish. Globefish is indispensable in sushi restaurants in the Kansai region.

イクラ軍艦巻き・*ikura gunkan-maki*
Salmon Roe Battleship Roll

イクラは鮭の卵を塩漬けにした食品で、卵がこぼれないように軍艦巻きにする。イクラはロシア語が語源で、魚卵全体を指す。

Salmon roe pickled in salt. They are eaten as battleship rolls to prevent the eggs from falling off. *Ikura* comes from the Russian word "ikra."

飛び子軍艦巻き・*tobiko gunkan-maki*
Flying-fish Roe Battleship Roll

飛び子は飛び魚(うお)の卵を塩漬けにした食品。飛び魚は、胸びれを広げて水上へ飛び出すことから、そう呼ばれる。

Flying-fish roe pickled in salt. They spread their pectoral fins and jump out of the water when they swim, which gave this fish its name.

ウニ軍艦巻き・*uni gunkan-maki*
Sea Urchin Battleship Roll

イガイガの体を割った内側にある生殖腺を食用にする。イクラとともに、代表的な軍艦巻き。

The gonads inside the thorny shell of the sea urchin is eaten in sushi. As with *ikura*, it is a popular ingredient for *gunkan-maki*.

蟹みそ軍艦巻き・*kani-miso gunkan-maki*
Crab Butter Battleship Roll

日本にはズワイガニ、タラバガニ、毛ガニなどがある。甲羅のなかにある内臓を蟹みそといい、軍艦巻きにする。蟹の身を添えたものもある。

There are many crabs in Japan, such as snow crabs, king crabs and hairy crabs. The internal organs of a crab are called *kani-miso* and are eaten as *gunkan-maki*. Some are served with crab flesh.

鉄火巻き・*tekka-maki*
Tuna Roll

鮪の細巻き（39頁）のこと。語源には諸説あり、鮪の身の色を赤く燃えた鉄「鉄火」に見立てたから、もしくは昔の博打場（鉄火場）で好まれたからという説もある。

Hoso-maki (page 39) of tuna. "*Tekka*" means "hot red iron," which is one etymology for this sushi, likening the red flesh of tuna to hot iron. Another is that this *tekka-maki* was popular in old-time gambling houses which were called *tekkaba*.

かっぱ巻き・*kappa-maki*
Cucumber Roll

胡瓜の細巻きのこと。「かっぱ」とは、くちばしと甲羅を持ち、頭上に水をたたえた皿をのせる日本古来の想像状の動物。胡瓜がかっぱの好物であったとされることからのネーミング。

Hoso-maki of cucumbers. A *kappa* is a mythological creature in Japan with a beak, a shell like a turtle and a plate with water on its head. It is said that they like cucumbers, which is why this *hoso-maki* is named *kappa-maki*.

太巻き・*futo-maki*
Thick Roll

海苔で酢飯と具材を包み、太めに巻いた寿司の一種。一般的な具材は、穴子、玉子、甘辛く煮たかんぴょう（ユウガオの果肉からつくる紐状の乾物）、椎茸、胡瓜、海老など。

Thick rolled sushi with vinegared rice and ingredients wrapped in *nori* (a sheet of dried seaweed). Common ingredients are *anago*, egg, sweet and salty simmered *kanpyo* (dried gourd shavings), shiitake mushrooms, cucumbers and prawns.

手巻き寿司・*temaki-zushi*
Hand-rolled Sushi

巻き簾を使わず、手で持てる大きさに海苔でひと巻きした寿司の一種。家庭では、めいめいが海苔を持ち、好みの材料を選んで巻く。

Hand-rolled (*te-maki*) sushi made without using a *makisu* (bamboo mat). In homes, everyone wraps whatever ingredients of sushi they prefer.

関西
Kansai-style

関東
Kanto-style

稲荷寿司・*inari-zushi*

Vinegared Rice Stuffed in a Bag of *Abura-age*

醬油や砂糖で甘辛く煮た油揚げのなかに、酢飯を詰めた寿司の一種。油揚げは、稲荷神（いなりのかみ）の使いである狐の好物とされ、「いなり」や「きつね」と呼ばれる。

Sushi made by cooking *abura-age* sweet and salty with soy sauce and sugar, then filling it with vinegared rice. *Abura-age* is said to be a favorite of foxes (*kitsune*), the messengers of the Inari god, which is why they are also called *inari* or *kitsune*.

押し寿司・*oshi-zushi*

Pressed Sushi

樽（たる）や桶などに酢飯と具材を重ね、おもしなどで上から圧（お）した寿司の一種。タネ（36頁）は鮭や鯖が一般的。柿の葉で包んだ柿の葉寿司も押し寿司の一つ。

Vinegared rice and ingredients pressed tightly in barrels or buckets by using weights. Salmon and mackerel are common for this type of sushi. *Kakinoha-zushi*, wrapped with persimmon leaves, is also an *oshi-zushi*.

ちらし寿司(関東)・*chirashi-zushi (in Kanto)*
Scattered Sushi with Fresh Ingredients

にぎり寿司にする新鮮なタネや玉子を、酢飯の上にきれいに並べたもの。タネを醬油につけながら食べる。

Fresh *tane* (ingredients of sushi) and *tamago* (egg) topped beautifully on vinegared rice. The *tane* are dipped in soy sauce when eating.

ちらし寿司(関西)・*chirashi-zushi (in Kansai)*
Scattered Sushi with Seasoned Iingredients

錦糸玉子(細く切った薄焼き玉子)、茹でた海老、甘辛く煮た椎茸や人参など、味付けをしたタネを酢飯の上に盛り付けたものをいう。

Seasoned ingredients such as *kinshi tamago* (fine slices of a thin sheet of egg), boiled prawn, sweet and salty simmered shiitake mushrooms and carrots topped on vinegared rice.

ダシの材料

和食の味を決めるのはダシ。鰹節や昆布でとるのが一般的だが、魚の煮干しや干し椎茸の戻し汁なども使う。

鰹節・*katsuobushi*
Dried Bonito

鰹の身を干し固めたもの。これを削って、熱湯で煮出してダシをとる。鰹節は、三枚におろした鰹の身を、よく煮てから燻製にして、室（むろ）でのカビつけと天日干しを繰り返して仕上げる。鰹節を花びらのように薄く削ったものを「花鰹」といい、トッピングとしても利用する。

Dried bonito (*katsuo*) is shaved and boiled in hot water for *dashi* (soup stock). *Katsuobushi* shaved thin like flower petals are called *hana-katsuo* ("*hana*" means "flower") and are used as toppings.

昆布・*kombu*
Dried *Kombu* Kelp

昆布を天日干しにしたもの。必要な大きさに切って水に入れ、沸騰する前に取り出す。日本料理店で使うダシは昆布と鰹節でとったものが一般的。北海道が主な産地で、真昆布、羅臼昆布、利尻昆布、日高昆布などの種類があり、それぞれに風味が異なる。

Kombu dried in the sun. For soup stock, they are cut in pieces, put in water and taken out before the water boils. In restaurants that specialize in Japanese cuisine, soup stock from *kombu* and *katsuobushi* are common. Mainly produced in Hokkaido Prefecture.

Ingredients of Soup Stock (*dashi*)

Dashi plays a vital role in *washoku* (Japanese cooking). Other than dried bonito shavings and *kombu*, which are most common, dried small sardines and dried shiitake mushrooms are also used.

鰯の煮干し・*iwashi no niboshi*
Dried Sardines

鰯を煮熟してから天日干ししたもの。カタクチイワシが代表的だが、鯵（あじ）や飛び魚（うお）などの小魚も原料とされる。飛び魚の煮干しでとったダシは「あごだし」と呼ばれる。

Boiled and sun-dried sardines. Japanese anchovies are most common, but small fish such as horse mackerels and flying-fish are also used. Soup stock taken from flying-fish is called *ago-dashi*.

干し椎茸・*hoshi-shiitake*
Dried Shiitake Mushroom

「どんこ」と呼ばれる肉厚の椎茸を乾燥させたもの。それを水に入れて戻した後の汁をダシに加える。戻した椎茸自身も料理の食材となる。

Dried *donko*, a type of thick shiitake mushroom. The mushrooms need to be soaked in water until they become tender, then the soaking liquid is added to the soup stock. The mushrooms are also used for cooking.

香味野菜と香辛料

日本料理は盛り付けの仕上げとして、香味野菜や香辛料をあしらって香りや色を添える。両方をあわせて「薬味（やくみ）」ともいう。

刺身のあしらい
Toppings for Sashimi

酢の物のあしらい
Toppings for Sunomono

Herbs and Spices (*komi-yasai* and *koshinryo*)

Herbs and spices are used to finish up a dish and to add flavor and color. They are called *yakumi*.

1
つま・*tsuma*
Garnish Served with Sashimi

刺身に添える香味野菜を指す。つまは「妻」の意味とされる。

"*Tsuma*" means "wife," because they stay by the sashimi's side.

2
けん・*ken*
Shredded Vegetables with Sashimi

刺身に添える千切りにした野菜を指す。大根が一般的で、ほかに胡瓜や茗荷（みょうが・66頁）も用いられる。けんは「剣」の意味とされる。

Daikon radish is most popular, and cucumbers or *myoga* (Japanese ginger; page 66) may also be used. In Japanese, "*ken*" means "sword."

3
辛み・*karami*
Spice

山葵（わさび・66頁）や生姜などの香辛料。「つま」に含めることもある。

Spices such as wasabi (page 66) and ginger are called *karami*. They may also be served as *tsuma*.

4
天盛り・*temmori*
Toppings of Dishes

煮物や酢の物を山形に盛り付けた上にそっとのせた香味野菜を指す。これは、まだ誰もこの料理に手をつけていないことを示す、客人への心配りにもなっている。

Herbs served on top of simmered dishes or *sunomono* (salad dressed with vinegar). It is a way of allowing the customers to know that the dish has not been touched by anyone.

椀物のあしらい
Toppings for Wanmono

1

吸口・*suikuchi*

Fragrant Garnish Added to *Wanmono*

盛り付けの最後にのせて、香りと彩りを添える、柚子（70-71頁）や木の芽（67頁）などのこと。

Yuzu (page 70-71) or *kinome* (page 67) which is topped last to finish up a dish. This adds scent and color to the dish.

2

椀種・*wandane*

Main Ingredient of *Wanmono*

椀物のメインの食材をいう。

The main ingredient in a lacquerware soup bowl (page 105).

3

椀づま・*wanzuma*

Seasonal Vegetables with *Wandane*

椀種に添える季節の野菜類などを指す。「つま」は妻の意味という。

The word "*zuma*" means "wife." (The "*zu*" here in "*zuma*" is a voiced consonant of "*tsu*" in "*tsuma*.")

4

吸地・*suiji*

Soup of *Wanmono*

椀物の汁を指す。澄まし汁（鰹節と昆布でとったダシに薄く味付けした汁）が多い。

The soup is oftentimes *sumashi-jiru* (lightly seasoned soup stock taken from *katsuobushi* and *kombu*).

山葵・*wasabi*
Wasabi

アブラナ科の植物ワサビの根茎。すりおろして香辛料として用いる。独特の高い香気と辛味を持ち、寿司、刺身、蕎麦などに欠かせない。

The root of the wasabi (Japanese horseradish) plant, of the Brassicaceae family. Grated and used as a spice. With its unique scent and sharp taste, it is a must-have for dishes such as sushi, sashimi and *soba*.

生姜・*shoga*
Ginger

ショウガ科の多年草の根茎。すりおろしたり（おろし生姜）、細かく刻んだり（刻み生姜）、千切りにしたり（針生姜）して、魚料理やそうめん（30頁）などに添える。生臭さを消す働きがあるので、特に青魚に適している。寿司屋では「がり」（39頁）としておなじみ。

Served with fish dishes or *somen* noodles (page 30) as *oroshi-shoga* (grated), *kizami-shoga* (cut in fine pieces) or *hari-shoga* (shredded like needles). Especially good with bluefish. Known as *gari* (page 39) in sushi restaurants.

茗荷・*myoga*
Japanese Ginger

ショウガ科の多年草。開花する前のつぼみ（花穂）の部分を千切りや輪切りにして、夏の料理に用いる。語源は諸説あるが、古くはその薫り高さから「芽香（めが）」と呼ばれ、転化したとされる。

A perennial plant in the Zingiberaceae family. The buds are taken before blooming, and are shredded or cut in rounds. Used for summer dishes.

木の芽・*kinome*

Buds of Japanese Pepper

ミカン科の低木サンショウ（山椒）の若芽をいう。春の椀物の吸口、天盛りに欠かせない存在。軽くたたき、香りを立たせてからのせる。実も食用として使う。

The young leaves of *sansho*, Japanese pepper. Essential as *suikuchi* and *tenmori* (toppings for Japanese dishes) for spring *wanmono*. Pressed slightly for more scent before topping. The seeds are also edible.

芽葱・*menegi*

Sprouts of Long Green Onion

ネギの若芽。ネギの種を密播きにし、芽吹いた直後に収穫する。

The seeds of long green onions are planted densely, and are harvested right after they sprout.

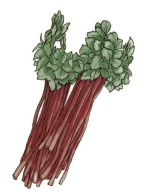

防風・*bofu*

Glehnia Littoralis

セリ科の多年草で、海辺の砂地に自生する「浜防風」の栽培種。正月や春先の一品に添えられる。

An agricultural species of the Glehnia littoralis which grows wild in sandy soils by the sea. They are served for the New Year and in the beginning of spring.

大葉・*oba*
青紫蘇・*ao-jiso*
Green Perilla

シソ科植物の紫蘇(しそ)は芽・花・葉・穂・実のすべてが香味野菜になる。青紫蘇と赤紫蘇があり、青紫蘇の葉が大葉と呼ばれる。赤紫蘇の葉は梅干しづくりに用いられる。

The bud, flower, leaf, ear and seed—all parts of the perilla are used as herbs. There are two kinds, green and red *shiso*. *Oba* is the leaf of the green perilla. Red perilla leaves are used for making *umeboshi* (pickled plums).

穂紫蘇・*ho-jiso*
Young Spikes of Perilla

紫蘇の若い穂。刺身のつま(63頁)だけでなく、天ぷらや酢の物、塩漬けなどにもする。

Served as *tsuma* (page 63) for sashimi, as tempura and *sunomono* (vinegared dishes). Also eaten pickled in salt.

花穂紫蘇・*hanaho-jiso*
Ear of *Shiso* Flower

咲きかけの花をつけた紫蘇の穂。刺身のつまとして盛られている場合、穂から花をしごいて醬油に落とすこともある。

The spikes of *shiso* with flowers about to bloom. When served as *tsuma* for sashimi, the flowers are sometimes dropped into the soy sauce.

青芽・*aome*

Young Buds of Green Perilla

青紫蘇の芽。刺身のつま、椀物の吸口(65頁)などに用いる。
Used for *tsuma* and for *suikuchi* (page 65).

紫芽・*murame*

Young Buds of Red Perilla

赤紫蘇の芽。青芽と同様、刺身のつまや、椀物の吸口などに用いる。
Like green perillas, they are used for *tsuma* and for *suikuchi*.

青柚子・*ao-yuzu*
青柚・*aoyu*
Green *Yuzu* Citrus

柑橘類の一つ、柚子。果汁はもちろん、皮をすりおろしたり、へぎ取ったりして、椀物の吸口(65頁)や天盛り(63頁)として用いる。

The fruit of *yuzu*, a citrus fruit. In addition to its juice, *yuzu* peels are also used for *suikuchi* (page 65) or *tenmori* (page 63) by grating or scraping them.

かぼす・*kabosu*
Kabosu Citrus

柑橘類の一つで大分県の特産品。果汁は酸味が強く、独特の風味がある。

A citrus fruit with a unique acidic taste. A specialty of Oita Prefecture.

すだち・*sudachi*
Sudachi Citrus

柚子、かぼすより小ぶりな柑橘類。徳島県の特産品。焼き魚や揚げ物などに絞って用いる。

A citrus fruit, smaller than *yuzu* and *kabosu*. A specialty of Tokushima Prefecture. Squeezed on grilled fish or deep-fried dishes.

へぎ柚子
Hegi-yuzu

刻み柚子
Kizami-yuzu

松葉柚子
Matsuba-yuzu

黄柚子・*ki-yuzu*

Yellow *Yuzu* Citrus

青柚子が秋に熟して黄色くなったもの。果汁はもちろん、皮をへぎ取ったり(へぎ柚子)、刻んだり(刻み柚子)、飾り切り(松葉柚子ほか)にして用いる。半分に割って果実を取り出し、なかに具材を詰めた「柚子釜」という料理がある。

Ao-yuzu that has become ripe and yellow in autumn. In addition to its juice, peels are used as scraped peels (*hegi-yuzu*), chopped peels (*kizami-yuzu*), and decorative cut peels (such as *matsuba-yuzu*, which are shaped like pine needles). There is also a dish called *yuzu-gama* which is made by cutting the *yuzu* in half, taking out the fruit and stuffing it with other ingredients.

山菜

山野に自生する食用植物のこと。早春に芽吹いたところをいただく。全国各地に、日本特有の山菜がある。

菜の花・*nanohana*
花菜・*hanana*
Canola Blossoms

アブラナ、もしくはアブラナの花の別名。つぼみの部分をお浸しや和え物にする。種から採った菜種油は食用になるが、昔は灯火などに使われ、搾りかすは肥料にされた。

Used for *ohitashi* (vegetables parboiled and soused in soup stock) or *aemono* (cooked vegetables with dressing). Although rapeseed oil is used for cooking these days, once it was used for lamplight. Oil lees were used as fertilizer.

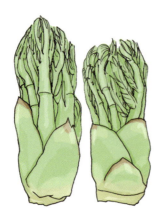

たらの芽・*taranome*
Buds of Japanese Angelica

高さ4〜5mになるタラノキの枝先に芽吹く新芽。天ぷらが定番。一度芽を摘んでもその横からまた芽が出るが、これを摘むと枝が枯れるといわれる。

The buds of Aralia elata, or the Japanese angelica tree, which grows up to 4-5 meters. Best eaten as tempura. New buds come out again after the first is picked, but it is said that the branch will die if this new shoot is taken.

Edible Wild Plants (*sansai*)

Edible wild plants in the fields and mountains. The buds and shoots that come out in early spring are eaten. *Sansai* indigenous to Japan can be found all over the country.

野蒜・*nobiru*

Wild Rocambole

ユリ科の多年草。蒜（ひる）は葱類の総称で、野蒜は人里近くに生えるため、昔から葱の代用とされてきた。鱗茎（りんけい）部分を生のまま、もしくは茹でてから味噌をつけて食べる。

A perennial plant in the Liliaceae family. Since they grow near human inhabitation, they have served as a substitute for long green onions. The bulb is eaten with miso, either raw or boiled.

萱草・*kanzo*

Hemerocallis Fulva

ユリ科の花萱草の若芽。ほのかな苦味と甘みがある。さっと茹でて、お浸しにしたり、ホタルイカなどの魚介類と酢味噌和えにしたりする。花は黄味がかった橙（だいだい）色で、「萱草色」という色の名前になっている。

The shoots of Hemerocallis fulva, a plant in the Liliaceae family. Parboiled and eaten as *ohitashi*, or as *aemono*, dressed in vinegared miso with fish or shellfish such as firefly squid. There is a color called *kanzo*, named after this plant's yellowish orange flower.

山独活・*yama-udo*
Wild *Udo*

独活は高さ2mにもなるウコギ科の多年草で、自生するものは特に「山独活」と呼んでいる。新芽と若葉は天ぷらや煮物にし、根茎は生のまま酢味噌で食べたり、むいた皮をきんぴらにする。

A perennial plant in the Araliaceae family that grows as high as 2 meters. Wild *udo* is called *yama-udo* (*udo* in the mountains). Young buds and leaves are eaten as tempura or *nimono* and roots are eaten raw. Peels are chopped in thin strips and stir-fried.

土筆・*tsukushi*
Spore Shoot of Field Horsetail

早春に生えるスギナの胞子茎。昔は「つくづくし」といった。筆の形に似ていることから「土筆」の漢字を当てる。お浸しや炒め物にする。

Field horsetail shoots that grow in early spring. They were traditionally called *tsukuzukushi*. Eaten as *ohitashi* (vegetables parboiled and soused in soup stock) or stir-fried.

蕨・*warabi*

Bracken

シダ植物で、若芽を「早蕨（さわらび）」といって珍重する。昔は根茎から取り出したデンプンを乾燥させて「わらび粉」をつくり、わらび餅の原料にした。

A type of fern. The young shoots are called *sawarabi*. Starch taken from the roots was dried to make *warabi* starch, which was then made into a Japanese confectionery called *warabi-mochi*. However, other kinds of starch are more common these days for *warabi-mochi*.

薇・*zemmai*

Osmunda

水気の多いところに生えるシダ植物。食用となる若芽はきれいな渦巻状になっている。その形から、弾力性に富むバネのことを日本では「ぜんまい」と呼ぶ。

A type of fern which grows in damp places. The edible young shoots all grow in beautiful spirals. Named after this shape, elastic springs are called *zenmai* in Japanese.

和菓子

日本独自に発展した菓子を和菓子といい、小豆餡や餅が使われているものが多い。和菓子は「生(なま)菓子」と「干(ひ)菓子」に大別され、製造方法や素材が異なる。

餡蜜・*ammitsu*
Agar-jelly Cubes with Sweet Bean Paste in Syrup

寒天、餡、赤えんどう豆、果物、餅などを盛り合わせて、黒蜜をかけたもの。餡をのせていないものを「蜜豆(みつまめ)」といい、江戸時代より売られていたという。

Kanten (agar-jelly), sweet red bean paste (*an*), *akaendo* (red peas), fruits and *mochi* (rice cake) served together in a bowl, with *kuromitsu* (brown sugar syrup) poured over them. Without the bean paste, the dessert is called *mitsumame*.

善哉・*zenzai*
Sweet Red Bean Soup with a Piece of Rice Cake

小豆に水と砂糖を加えて煮込み、餅や白玉団子などを入れたもの。煮汁をきれいに濾(こ)したものは一般に(特に関西では)、「汁粉」と呼ばれる。関東では、餅に汁気のない餡をのせたものを善哉と呼ぶことがある。

Mochi or *shiratama-dango* (rice-flour dumplings) served in sweet soup made by cooking adzuki beans with water and sugar. When the soup has been strained to make it smooth, it is called *shiruko*, especially in Kansai.

Confectionery (*wagashi*)

The most popular ingredients are sweet red bean paste (*an*) and rice cake (*mochi*). *Wagashi* can be roughly divided into two categories according to the ways that they are produced and their ingredients: *namagashi* (raw) and *higashi* (dried).

羊羹・*yokan*
Bar of Jellied Sweet Bean Paste

寒天を水で煮溶かし、砂糖と餡を加えて練り、細長い型に流し固めたもの。これを「練羊羹」というのに対して、寒天の量が少なくてやわらかいものを「水羊羹」、練った餡に小麦粉や葛粉などを加えて蒸し固めたものを「蒸し羊羹」という。

Made by dissolving *kanten* in water over heat, kneading it with sugar and sweet red bean paste, then pouring the mixture into a long and narrow container to let is set. While this type of *yokan* is called *neri-yokan* (kneaded *yokan*), a softer type with less *kanten* is called *mizu-yokan* (water *yokan*).

金鍔・*kintsuba*
Baked Sweet Bean Paste Coated with Thin Dough

四角もしくは円形に固めた餡に、小麦粉の水溶きをつけて焼いたもの。金鍔の鍔とは日本刀の持ち手と刀身の間に差し込む鉄の輪のこと。その形に似ていたことからのネーミングとされる。

Square or round-shaped sweet bean paste, coated with thin wheat-flour dough then baked. The kanji for "*tsuba*" indicates an iron ring held between the blade and the hilt of a Japanese sword. *Kintsuba* resembled this shape, which was the origin for its name.

薯蕷饅頭・*joyo-manju*
Bun Stuffed with Sweet Bean Paste

すりおろした薯蕷芋(とろろいも/山芋、つくね芋など)に米粉などを混ぜて蒸した皮で、餡を包んだ菓子。高級という意味を含めて「上用饅頭」と書くこともある。

Steamed buns made from grated yam (such as *yama-imo*, *tsukune-imo*, etc.) mixed with rice flour, filled with sweet red bean paste.

豆大福・*mame-daifuku*
Rice Cake Stuffed with Sweet Bean Paste

餅の皮で餡を包んだものを「大福餅」といい、餅に赤えんどう豆を入れたものを「豆大福」という。生地に蓬(よもぎ)を加えた「蓬大福(草大福)」、餡に苺を入れた「苺大福」なども人気。

Sweet red bean paste wrapped in *mochi* (rice cake) is called *daifuku-mochi*, while ones with red peas in the *mochi* are called *mame-daifuku* ("*mame*" means "peas"). Other types include *yomogi-daifuku* (*kusa-daifuku*) with *yomogi* (mugwort leaves) mixed in the *mochi* and *ichigo-daifuku* with a strawberry inside the bean paste.

今川焼き・*imagawayaki*
大判焼き・*obanyaki*
回転焼き・*kaitenyaki*
Pancake Stuffed with Sweet Bean Paste

左右二つ折りの焼き型を使って、小麦粉・水・砂糖・卵を混ぜた生地を焼き、餡を包んだ菓子。地方によって「今川焼き」、「大判焼き」、「回転焼き」などと呼ばれる。

Made by using a two-fold mold. Batter made from wheat-flour, water, sugar and eggs is baked with this mold, then filled with sweet red bean paste.

どら焼き・*dorayaki*
三笠・*mikasa*
Two Pancakes with Sweet Bean Paste in Between

小麦粉・卵・砂糖を混ぜた生地を丸く焼き、2枚の皮で餡を挟んだ菓子。打楽器の銅鑼（どら）と似ていることからの名前。関西では奈良の三笠山を連想させるため、「三笠」とも呼ばれる。

Sweet red bean paste sandwiched between two pancakes made from wheat-flour, eggs and sugar. Named after the gong, which is called *dora*.

最中・*monaka*
Wafers Cakes Stuffed with Sweet Bean Paste

餅を薄く焼いた皮2枚の間に餡を挟んだ菓子。十五夜の満月を「最中（もなか）の月」といい、名月に見立てたこの菓子を「最中」と呼んだとされる。

Sweet red bean paste sandwiched between two thin wafers made from *mochi*. This confectionery was likened to the harvest moon which is called *monaka no tsuki*.

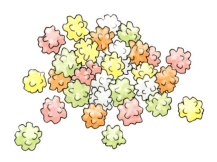

金平糖・*kompeito*
Sugar Candy

回転する大きな釜を用いて、芥子の実に砂糖蜜を何度もかけてつくる砂糖の結晶。ポルトガル伝来の南蛮菓子の一つで、砂糖菓子を意味するポルトガル語のconfeitoから付いた名前。

Made in a large rotating tub, by crystallizing liquid sugar around a poppy seed core. Originally from Portugal, this confectionery was named from the Portuguese word "confeito" which means "candy."

有平糖・*aruheito*
Sugar Candy Mixed with Starch Syrup

砂糖を煮詰めて着色した飴菓子の一種。その季節を象徴するさまざまな物に形づくられる。ポルトガル伝来の南蛮菓子の一つで、alfeloaもしくはalfenimという砂糖菓子が原型とされる。絵は「千代結び」という形。

A type of candy made by boiling down sugar and adding coloring. Made into various shapes that represent each season. Originally from Portugal, it is said that *aruheito* comes from a candy which is called either "alfeloa" or "alfenim." The picture here shows a shape called *chiyomusubi*, which means an "everlasting bond."

落雁・*rakugan*

Pressed Cake Made of Rice Flour and Sugar

砂糖と水飴を溶かした液に米や麦などの粉を加えて混ぜ、木型に詰めて成型し、取り出した干菓子。語源は諸説あり、中国の菓子「軟落甘（なんらくかん）」にちなむという説もある。

A *higashi* made by adding flour such as rice flour and barley flour to a mixture of sugar and starch syrup. This mixture is poured into a wooden mold then taken out after it is set.

松風・*matsukaze*

Baked Cake Made from Sugar and Wheat Flour

小麦粉・砂糖・水などを混ぜ合わせた生地を平らにし、芥子の実を散らして焼いた菓子。薄い煎餅状のものもあれば、絵のようなカステラ風のものもある。京都では白味噌を混ぜた「味噌松風」が多い。

Batter made from wheat flour, sugar and water, sprinkled with poppy seeds and baked. Some are thin like *senbei* (rice crackers) while others are baked like sponge cakes as shown in the picture. In Kyoto, the most popular ones are *miso-matsukaze* with white miso mixed in.

季節の和菓子

日本の菓子は、それが季節の風物を象徴していること、年中行事ごとに特定の菓子が存在するところに最大の特徴がある。ここでは12か月の代表的な菓子を紹介する。

1月　January

花びら餅・*hanabira-mochi*

Rice Cake with Burdock and Miso-flavored Sweet Bean Paste

薄い求肥（ぎゅうひ）※でごぼうと味噌餡を包んだ正月の茶席菓子。宮中の正月行事に食する「菱葩（ひしはなびら）」にルーツがあり、ごぼうは鮎を見立てている。餅と味噌の組み合わせから「包み雑煮」という異名もある。　※水を加えてこねた餅粉を蒸し、砂糖を加えて練ったもの。

A New Year's *wagashi*, served in tea ceremonies. Burdock and sweet bean paste with miso, wrapped in thin *gyuhi**. The burdock represents the sweetfish that was eaten in the Heian court's New Year rituals.
*Glutinous rice flour mixed with water and steamed, before kneading with sugar.

2月　February

鶯餅・*uguisu-mochi*

Rice Cake Coated with Green Soybean Flour

求肥（ぎゅうひ）で餡を包み、青きな粉をまぶした菓子。その色が、2月に梅の木でさえずる鶯を思わせる。

Sweet red bean paste wrapped in *gyuhi*, sprinkled with green soybean flour. Its color makes one think of Japanese bush warblers (*uguisu*) singing on the branches of *ume* (Japanese plum) trees in February.

Seasonal Confectionery

The unique characteristic of Japanese confectionery lies in how each sweet is associated with a season and that special treats exist for each annual event. Here, typical confectioneries for each of the 12 months are introduced.

3月　March

草餅・*kusa-mochi*
蓬餅・*yomogi-mochi*
Rice Cake Mixed with Mugwort

茹でた蓬の若葉を加えた餅皮で、餡を包んだ菓子。3月に芽吹く蓬は「餅草」とも呼ばれる。蓬餅は3月3日の雛祭り(132頁)の祝い菓子にも用いられる。

Mochi (rice cake) with boiled *yomogi* leaves mixed in, filled with sweet red bean paste. The sprouts of *yomogi* that come out in March are also known as *mochi-kusa* ("*kusa*" means "grass"). *Yomogi-mochi* is a celebratory confectionery for the Girls' Doll Festival on March 3rd (page 132).

4月　April

関西
Kansai-style

関東
Kanto-style

桜餅・*sakura-mochi*
Rice Cake Wrapped in a Cherry Leaf

塩漬けにした桜の葉で包んだ菓子。餡を、蒸した道明寺粉(どうみょうじこ・もち米を蒸して乾燥させたもの)で包む関西風と、小麦粉を薄く焼いた皮で包む関東風がある。

Confectionery wrapped in a salt-pickled cherry leaf. In Kansai, *domyoji-ko* (flour made by steaming and drying glutinous rice) is used to make the *mochi* which is then filled with sweet red bean paste. In Kanto, dough made from wheat flour is baked thin and wrapped around the bean paste.

5月　May

落とし文・*otoshibumi*
Confectionery Shaped Like Rolled-up Leaves

オトシブミという甲虫は、5月頃、葉を巻いてつくったゆりかごのなかに卵を産む。このゆりかごを形づくった菓子。公然とはいえないことを書いて、わざと路上に落としておいた手紙に似ていたことから甲虫にオトシブミの名前が付いた。

In May, leaf-rolling weevils (*otoshibumi*) lay eggs inside cradles they make by rolling up leaves. *Otoshibumi* is a confectionery likened to this cradle. Leaf-rolling weevils are called *otoshibumi*.

6月　June

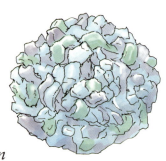

紫陽花金団・*ajisai-kinton*
Kinton Likened to the Flowers of the Hydrangea

6月に咲く紫陽花（あじさい）を表した菓子。着色したそぼろ状の餡を、餡玉の周囲に付けたものを金団（きんとん）といい、さまざまな植物や風景を表現することができる。

Like the flowers of the hydrangea that bloom in June. *Kinton* refers to confectionery with colored crumbly sweet bean paste coated around a small ball of sweet bean paste. Various plants and scenery can be expressed with a *kinton*.

7月　July

葛饅頭・*kuzu-manju*
Bun with a Bean Paste Filling Covered with Kudzu Starch

葛粉を煮溶かした透明感のある皮で、餡を包んだ菓子。夏の和菓子は葛を使ったものが多い。葛粉は、マメ科のつる性多年草である葛の根からとるデンプンだが、近年は希少品になっている。

Many summer *wagashi* use translucent kudzu starch buns. Kudzu starch is taken from the roots of kudzu (Japanese arrowroot) which is a perennial creeper in the Fabaceae family. It has become a rare product in recent years.

8月　August

水（有平糖）・*mizu (aruheito)*
Sugar Candy Representing the Flow of Water

砂糖を煮詰めて着色した有平糖（80頁）で、水の流れを表した干菓子。

Aruheito (page 80) representing the flow of water. A type of *higashi* (Japanese dried confectionery).

9月　September

―
萩の餅・*hagi no mochi*
おはぎ・*ohagi*

Glutinous Rice Ball Coated with Sweet Bean Paste

餅米と米を混ぜて蒸したものを、餡で包んだ菓子。秋の彼岸（秋分の日の前後）に食べる菓子で、その頃に咲く萩の花になぞらえて「萩の餅」という。春の彼岸（春分の日の前後）にも同様の菓子を食べるが、こちらは牡丹になぞらえて「ぼた餅（牡丹餅）」と呼び分けることもある。

Glutinous rice and non-glutinous rice mixed together and steamed to make dumplings, which is then covered with sweet bean paste. Since they are eaten in the autumn equinoctial week, they are called *hagi no mochi* after the plant *hagi* (Japanese bush clover), which flowers in autumn. They are also eaten in the vernal equinoctial week, and their name changes to *bota-mochi* (*botan-mochi*), after the *botan* (peony) flowers of the season.

10月　October

―
吹き寄せ・*fukiyose*

An Assortment of Dried Confectionery Representing the Autumn Season

色づいた木の葉や木の実などを形づくった干菓子を寄せ集め、秋の風情を表したもの。「吹き寄せ」とは、秋風で落葉が一か所に集まることをいう。また、数種類の具材を盛り合わせた秋の料理も「吹き寄せ」と呼ぶ。

An assortment of *higashi* shaped like colored leaves and nuts, representing the autumn season. *Fukiyose* is a word which expresses how fallen leaves gather in one spot by the autumn wind. Autumn dishes with several different ingredients served together are also called *fukiyose*.

11月　November

—
亥の子餅・*inoko-mochi*
玄猪餅・*gencho-mochi*
Rice Cake Representing the Baby Boar

餡を求肥で包んで猪（亥）の子どもを表した菓子。昔は、猪の多産にあやかり無病息災・子孫繁栄を願う、旧暦10月はじめの亥の日の行事で食べられた。茶道では11月に食べる菓子の定番。

Sweet bean paste wrapped in *gyuhi* (pege 82), likened to a baby boar. Once, this confectionery was eaten in rituals where people wished for good health and many happy descendants, after how boars bear many babies. Today, in the tea ceremony, it is a classic confectionery of November.

12月　December

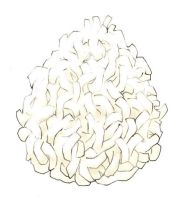

—
雪餅・*yuki-mochi*
Snow-white *Kinton*

大和芋や百合根からつくる餡を使って、雪のように真っ白に仕上げた金団（＝餡玉の周囲に着色したそぼろ状の餡をつけた菓子）。

Snow-white *kinton* which uses sweet bean paste made from Japanese yam or lily bulbs.

茶

日本の茶といえば緑茶。紅茶や烏龍茶との違いは、茶葉を発酵させないところ。作り方によってさまざまな種類がある。

煎茶・*sencha*
Green Tea

摘んだ葉を蒸し、揉みながら乾燥させた茶。湯を注ぎ、浸出した茶を飲む。緑茶のなかで最も一般的な飲み物。

Picked leaves are steamed then dried to make *sencha*. Pour hot water over the leaves and let them steep before drinking. *Sencha* is the most common type of green tea.

玉露・*gyokuro*
Green Tea of the Highest Quality

製法は煎茶と同じだが、茶畑に覆いをして日光を遮ることで旨みを増した茶葉を用いる高級茶。低温の湯を少量注ぎ、じっくりと淹れると、香り高くて甘みのある緑茶になる。

Though produced in the same way as *sencha*, this is a more expensive tea which uses tea leaves with more umami, made by shading the plantations to shut out sunlight.

抹茶・*matcha*
Powdered Green Tea

茶畑に覆いをして日光を遮ることで旨みを増した茶葉を粉末にしたもの。湯を注ぎ、茶筅(113頁)で攪拌(かくはん)してから飲む。

Umami-rich tea leaves made by shading the plantations are grinded into powder to produce *matcha*. Prepared by pouring hot water over the powder and blending it with a *chasen* (page 113).

Tea (*cha*)

Green tea is the most popular Japanese tea. It can be distinguished from black tea and oolong tea in that it does not undergo fermentation. There are various types of green tea, which are distinguishable by now how they are produced.

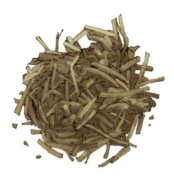

焙じ茶・*hojicha*
番茶・*bancha*
Roasted Green Tea

摘み残りの硬い茶葉でつくる煎茶を「番茶」という。番茶を焙煎させたものを「焙じ茶」といい、こうばしい香りが特徴。焙じ茶のことを番茶という地域もある。

Bancha is a type of *sencha*, made from coarse tea leaves that were left unpicked. *Hojicha*, made by roasting *bancha*, has a roasted aroma.

玄米茶・*gemmaicha*
Green Tea Mixed Roasted Popped Rice

炒った玄米を緑茶などに加えたもの。こうばしい香りで、カフェインが少ない。

Roasted *genmai* (brown rice) added to green tea. This tea has a fragrant roasted aroma, and little caffeine is contained.

茎茶・*kukicha*
雁が音・*karigane*
Green Tea Made of Stalks

玉露や煎茶の仕上げ工程で、新芽の茎だけを集めたもの。若々しい香りとさっぱりした味わいが特徴。茎の形が、雁が海上で羽を休めるために乗る小枝に似ていることから名が付いたとされる。

Young stalks are sorted out in the finishing process of producing *gyokuro* or *sencha* to make this tea. This tea has a fresh aroma and refreshing taste.

酒

近年、世界的にも人気の高い日本酒。しかし日本には焼酎や泡盛といったアルコール飲料もあり、全国各地にたくさんの蔵元(製造所)が存在する。

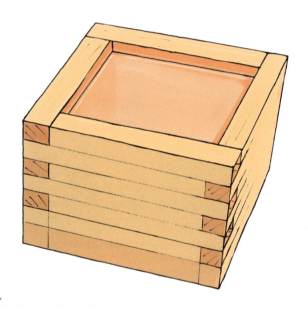

日本酒・*nihonshu*
Sake

米・水・米麹を原料にして、酵母の働きで発酵させてつくる醸造酒。アルコール度は15〜16度。「純米酒」と「本醸造酒」があり、「本醸造酒」には醸造用アルコールが添加されている。温めて飲むものを「燗酒」という。祝い事などのとき、大きな木樽に入れた酒を絵のような枡(ます)に汲んで飲むことがある。

Sake made by fermentation, with rice, water and *koji* (malted rice). Its alcohol content is 15 to 16%. When heated, it is called *kan-zake*. For celebrations, sake in large wooden barrels is drunk in square wooden containers as shown in the picture. These container are called *masu*.

Alcoholic Drink (sake)

Sake has become popular all over the world in recent years. However, Japan has other kinds of alcohol such as *shochu* and *awamori*, and there are numerous breweries all over the country.

焼酎・*shochu*
Distilled Spirits

主に米・麦・さつまいもなどを原料としてつくられる蒸留酒。九州地方が主産地。アルコール度は20度か25度のものが多く、水や氷、お湯などで割って飲むのが一般的。絵は「黒ぢょか」と呼ばれる専用の酒器で、焼酎と水を入れ、湯せんなどで温める。

A type of distilled liquor made mainly from rice, barley and sweet potatoes. Mainly produced in the Kyushu region. Its alcohol content is generally 20 to 25%, and it is usually mixed with water, ice cubes or hot water when drinking.

泡盛・*awamori*
Distilled Liquor Made From Rice

タイ米を原料として、黒麹菌を用いて蒸留させた沖縄県特産の焼酎。一般流通品はアルコール度30度だが、40度を超えるものもある。ストレート、ロック、水割りで飲むのが一般的。絵は「カラカラ」と呼ばれる酒器で、沖縄でよく用いられる。

A type of *shochu* from Okinawa Prefecture, made by distilling Jasmine rice with black *koji* mold. Although the alcohol content of the most common ones in the market is around 30%, some go over 40%. Generally enjoyed straight up, on the rocks or with water.

和食の調味料
Seasonings for *Washoku*

醤油・*shoyu*　　Soy Sauce

大豆と小麦に麴菌を加えて麴をつくり、塩水を加えて発酵・熟成させたもの。「こいくち」と「うすくち」があり、「こいくち」が一般的に認知されている醤油のこと。「うすくち」は、料理の見た目をきれいにするために、塩水を高濃度にして色を薄く仕上げた醤油。

Produced by adding aspergillus to soybeans and wheat, in order to make soy sauce malt, which is then fermented and matured by adding salt water. There are two types of soy sauce—*koikuchi* and *usukuchi*. *Koikuchi* is the soy sauce that is generally used. *Usukuchi* is soy sauce that has high concentration of salt and lighter color, therefore seasoning food without turning its color dark, used for aesthetic reasons.

味噌・*miso*　　Miso/Soybean Paste

大豆に麴と塩を混ぜ合わせて、熟成させたもの。米麴を使った「米味噌」が広く流通している。ほかに、麦麴を使う「麦味噌」、麦麴と米麴を使う「合わせ味噌」、大豆と塩だけでつくる「豆味噌」がある。

Made by maturing soybeans with aspergillus and salt. *Kome-miso* (rice miso) that uses rice malt is common. Other types include *mugi-miso* (barley miso) which uses barley malt, *awase-miso* (mixed miso) which uses barley malt and rice malt, and *mame-miso* (bean miso) which is made only from soybean and salt.

酒・*sake*　　Sake

日本酒のこと。料理用につくられた酒もある。90頁参照。

Japanese alcohol. Some sake is made specifically for cooking. Please refer to page 90.

みりん・*mirin*　　Sweet Sake for Seasoning

蒸した餅米に、米麴と醸造用アルコールを加えて糖化・熟成させた、甘みのある酒のような調味料。これを「本みりん」といい、アルコール度は14度ほどで酒類に分類される。近年は、醸造用アルコールを使わない「みりん風調味料」が一般的になっている。

A sweet sake-like seasoning, made from steamed glutinous rice, which is saccharified and matured by adding rice malt and distilled alcohol to it. This is called *hon-mirin*. When its alcohol content goes up to around 14%, it is considered sake. In recent years, *mirin*-like seasonings without distilled alcohol have become more common.

ポン酢・*ponzu*　　Citrus-based Soy Sauce

柚子、かぼす、すだち（70-71頁）など柑橘類の絞り汁に、醤油、ダシ、みりんなどを加えて調味したもの。鍋や蒸し物などのつけ汁として使用することが多い。語源はオランダ語で柑橘類を表す「ポンス（pons）」。

Juice of citrus fruits such as *yuzu*, *kabosu* or *sudachi* (pages 70 to 71), seasoned with soy sauce, soup stock, *mirin*, etc. Often used as dipping sauce for hotpots or steamed dishes. Derived from the Dutch word "pons" which indicates citrus fruits.

食器
TABLEWARE

磁器

主に白色の土や鉱物を原料に、うわぐすりをかけて焼いたガラス質の焼き物。吸水性がなく、透明感のある肌が特徴。

青磁・*seiji*
Blue Porcelain

花瓶、茶器、皿などに使われている青くて透明感のある磁器。うわぐすりに含まれるわずかな鉄分が熱に反応して青色になる。中国で製造が始まり、その製品と技法は日本や朝鮮半島にも伝わった。

A type of translucent blue *jiki*. Mainly used for flower vases, tea things and plates. The little iron contained in the glaze reacts to heat, which gives this porcelain its blue color. First produced in China, this *jiki* and its production techniques spread to Japan and the Korean Peninsula.

白磁・*hakuji*
White Porcelain

洋食器、和食器に最も多く見られる白い磁器。白色の素地に、鉄分のない透明のうわぐすりをかけ、高温で焼き上げる。中国で青磁より後代に製造が始まり、日本では江戸時代初期（17世紀初頭）に九州の有田で焼成ができるようになった。

This is the type of porcelain seen most in both Western and Japanese plates. White clay is finished with a transparent glaze that does not contain iron, which is then baked in high temperature. *Hakuji* originated in China after the times of *seiji*. In Japan, *hakuji* production started in Arita in Kyushu, in the beginning of the 17th century.

Porcelain (*jiki*)

Mainly made from white clay and minerals, *jiki* is a vitreous glazed pottery. It does not absorb water, and has a translucent surface.

染付・*sometsuke*
Blue and White Porcelain

白地に青い模様がある磁器。白い素地の上にコバルト顔料で模様を描き、透明のうわぐすりをかけて焼く。原産地の中国では「青花（せいか）」と呼ばれる。日本では伊万里焼（96頁）が世界的に有名。

A white *jiki* with blue designs. Cobalt pigments are used to draw the designs, over which transparent glaze is applied. In China where *sometsuke* originally comes from, it is called *seika* with the kanji characters for "blue" and "flower." *Imari-yaki* (page 96) in Japan is a world-famous *sometsuke*.

色絵・*iroe*
Overglaze Enamels

白地に赤・緑など二色以上の色ぐすりで上絵付けをした、華やかな磁器。1640年代に有田焼（96頁）の技術革新が行われ、色絵磁器がつくれるようになった。関西では京都の清水焼（97頁）も有名。

A gorgeous white *jiki* with overglaze paintings in more than two colors, such as red and green. In the 1640's, technical innovations of *arita-yaki* (page 96) led to the producing of *iroe jiki*. In Kansai, *kiyomizu-yaki* (page 97) is a well-known example of this type of *jiki*.

伊万里焼・*imari-yaki*／有田焼・*arita-yaki*
Imari Ware/Arita Ware

主に佐賀県有田でつくられる染付と色絵磁器。有田では17世紀初期に磁土が発見され、中国風の染付を製造するようになった。雪のような白地と繊細な絵付けが特徴の染付は、海外でも人気を博し、伊万里港から世界へ輸出されたことから「伊万里」がブランド名となった。その後に開発されたカラフルな色絵磁器も、透き通った白い肌と美しい絵付けで世界を魅了した。現在の和食器にも好んで使われている。

Sometsuke and *iroe* mainly made in Arita, Saga Prefecture. In Arita, porcelain clay was found in the early 17th century, which led to the production of Chinese *sometsuke*. *Sometsuke*, with its snow-white surface and delicate painting, gained reputation overseas. Since it was shipped to the world from Imari Port, *Imari* became its brand name. Afterwards, the colorful *iroe jiki* was made, which also fascinated people all over the world with its white translucent surface and beautiful paintings. It is favored today for Japanese tableware.

清水焼・*kiyomizu-yaki*
Kiyomizu Ware

京都でつくられる磁器。清水寺付近で焼かれていたことからのネーミング。もともと陶器に絵付けをしていたが、有田焼の磁器の技術を導入してから、華やかな色絵磁器が製造されるようになった。関西の和食器は清水焼が多い。

A type of *jiki* made in Kyoto. Originally made near Kiyomizu-dera Temple, which gave its name. After the technique for making *arita-yaki* porcelain was introduced, colorful *iroe jiki* production replaced painted ceramic ware. Most Japanese tableware in Kansai is *kiyomizu-yaki* porcelain.

九谷焼・*kutani-yaki*
Kutani Ware

主に石川県九谷で絵付けをした陶器と磁器。九谷焼独特の渋い色調が特徴で、古いものでは、赤・黄・緑・紫・紺青の5色を使った「九谷五彩」、赤を除く4色を余白を残さず塗り込めた「青手(あおで)」の飾り皿が有名。食器としては皿や鉢が多い。

Ceramics and porcelain painted in Kutani, Ishikawa Prefecture. The colors of *kutani-yaki* characteristically have a faint tone. Well-known *kutani-yaki* from the old days are the ornamental plates with five colors: red, yellow, green, purple and Prussian blue; or with four colors, excluding the red. As for everyday use *kutani-yaki*, plates and bowls are the main products.

陶器

粘土からつくる陶器には、素地(きじ)の上にうわぐすりをかけてから焼くものと、かけないで焼く焼締(やきし)めがある。日本各地に窯場があるが、ここでは代表的なものを紹介する。

織部焼・*oribe-yaki*
Oribe-style Mino Ware

岐阜県でつくられる「美濃焼(みのやき)」の一種。古田織部(1543〜1615)という武将にちなんだネーミング。緑色と黒みがかった幾何学模様の組み合わせが特徴で、料理店の和食器に好まれる。

A type of *mino-yaki* produced in Gifu Prefecture. Named after a military chief called Furuta Oribe (1543 to 1615). It is identifiable by its green and blackish geometrical patterns. Favored as Japanese tableware in restaurants.

志野焼・*shino-yaki*
Shino-style Mino Ware

美濃焼の一種。土がやわらかく、白いうわぐすりがたっぷりかかっているのが特徴。絵付けがあるものを「絵志野」といい、「卯花墻(うのはながき)」という名前の絵志野の抹茶茶碗は、日本の国宝になっている。

Another type of *mino-yaki*. Soft clay is used, with plenty of white glaze. Called *eshino* (painted *shino*) when painted. An *eshino matcha* bowl named Unohanagaki has been designated as a national treasure.

Ceramics (*toki*)

Ceramics made from clay can be classified in two: with or without glaze. Here we will introduce some of the most well-known ceramics in Japan.

信楽焼・*shigaraki-yaki*
Shigaraki Ware

主に滋賀県信楽でつくられる焼締め陶器。ほんのり赤みを帯びた土そのもののざらっとした肌触りが特徴で、花瓶や大皿、大鉢に向いている。笠をかぶったたぬきの置物が名物。

High-fired ceramics without glaze, mainly made in Shigaraki, Shiga Prefecture. They have a rough surface that comes from the slight red clay used to make this ceramic. Good for flower vases, large plates and large flower pots. Ceramic racoon dog figurines with bamboo hats made from *shigaraki-yaki* are well-known throughout Japan.

伊賀焼・*iga-yaki*
Iga Ware

主に三重県伊賀でつくられる焼締め陶器。高温で焼かれることによって、降りかかった薪の灰が緑色のガラス質（ビードロと呼ばれる）となったり、黒く焦げたりする荒々しさが魅力。耐火度が高いので、土鍋に向いている。

High-fired ceramics without glaze, mainly made in Iga, Mie Prefecture. Since they are baked in hot temperatures, firewood ashes that fall on the pottery form a glass-like glaze called *bidoro* or create black burns, which are both characteristic of *iga-yaki*.

常滑焼・*tokoname-yaki*
Tokoname Ware

主に愛知県常滑でつくられる焼締め陶器。鉄分の多いなめらかな粘土が特徴で、高温で焼き締めると赤褐色になる。これを朱泥（しゅでい）といい、朱泥の急須は常滑焼の特産品の一つになっている。

High-fired ceramics without glaze, mainly made in Tokoname, Aichi Prefecture. Made from smooth clay containing a lot of iron that becomes reddish brown when baked in hot temperatures. *Tokoname-yaki* is well-known for these *shudei* (red clay) teapots.

備前焼・*bizen-yaki* / 伊部焼・*imbe-yaki*
Bizen Ware/Imbe Ware

主に岡山県備前市伊部でつくられる焼締め陶器。鉄分を含む茶褐色の土を使った、素朴なたたずまいが魅力となっている。生産量の多い焼き物の産地の一つ。

High-fired ceramics without glaze, mainly made in Imbe, Bizen City, Okayama Prefecture. They are notable for their simple appearance, made from dark reddish brown clay containing iron. Bizen City is one of the areas in Japan that produces a large amount of ceramics.

萩焼・*hagi-yaki*
Hagi Ware

主に山口県萩でつくられる陶器。白い粘土と淡いうわぐすりを用いたやさしい肌が特徴。使い込むうちに水を吸って表情が変化する。湯飲みに好まれる焼き物の一つ。

Ceramics mainly made in Hagi, Yamaguchi Prefecture. Made from white clay and light-toned glaze, which gives it its graceful appearance. It absorbs water over time, meaning its beauty changes as it ages. Favored as teacups.

唐津焼・*karatsu-yaki*
Karatsu Ware

主に佐賀県唐津でつくられる陶器。絵付けしたものを「絵唐津」という。唐津焼には土肌を生かしたものから、うわぐすりを使ったものまで多様な技法があり、近年まで九州地方では陶磁器を総称して「唐津物」というほど、流通していた。

Ceramics mainly made in Karatsu, Saga Prefecture. When painted, they are called *ekaratsu*. Various techniques exist for *karatsu-yaki*, such as those that highlight the features of the clay by not using glaze, and those with glaze. They were very popular to the extent that until quite recently, pottery in general was referred to as *karatsu-mono* in Kyushu.

器

和食では、料理によってさまざまな形の器を使い分ける。ここでは代表的な食器と酒器の名前を紹介する。

四方皿・*yoho-zara* ／ 角皿・*kaku-zara*
Square Plate

正方形の四角い皿。「しほう皿」ともいうが、「よほう皿」と呼ぶことが多い。

A square-shaped plate ("*zara*" is the same as "*sara*" which means "plate." The pronunciation alters depending on which word precedes it).

長皿・*naga-zara*
Rectangular Plate

長方形の皿。焼き魚や前菜などを盛り付けることが多い。

Used mainly for serving grilled fish or appetizers.

俎板皿・*manaita-zara*
Flat Rectangular Plate

俎板(まないた)のように平らで横に長い皿。底(裏側)の左右に小さな脚がついているものもある。

A flat rectangular plate, shaped like a *manaita* (cutting board). Some have short legs attached to both sides on the back of the plate.

Tableware

In *washoku* (Japanese cooking), plates that come in various shapes are used for different types of dishes. Here, we will introduce some of the most popular tableware used in Japanese cuisine.

向付・*mukozuke*
Mukozuke Bowl

刺身や和え物などを入れる小鉢。本来は、茶道の食事「懐石」で、飯椀と汁椀の向こうに置く酒肴（しゅこう）、もしくはその器のことをいう。

A small bowl for serving sashimi or *aemono* (dressed dishes). Originally the name of a bowl used in *kaiseki* cuisine, in the tea ceremony.

なます皿・*namasu-zara*
Namasu Plate

少し深めの丸皿。古い伊万里の器（96頁）に用いる名前で、「なます」は酢の物のこと。

A round bowl. This name is used to indicate old *Imari* plates (page 96). *Namasu* refers to *sunomono* (vinegared dishes).

手付鉢・*tetsukibachi*
Dish with Handle

その名の通り、持ち手のついた鉢。持ち手はあくまで装飾なので、持たないほうがよい。

The handle is there solely for decoration; therefore it should not be held.

片口・*katakuchi*
Lipped Bowl

注ぎ口が1つだけついた鉢。本来は汁物や酒などの液体を注ぎ分ける用途の器だが、料理を盛り付けると食器になる。

Originally used as a pitcher for soup or sake. It can also be used to serve other dishes.

割山椒・*warizansho*
Cup with Three Slits

器の縁に3つの切れ目が入った器。山椒の実が割れたような形に見えることからのネーミング。少量の珍味や酒肴を入れる。

A cup with three slits around its edges. It is named *warizansho* because it resembles popped Japanese pepper (sansho) seeds, which are called *warizansho*. Used for serving small amounts of delicacies or things to nibble on while drinking.

塗椀・*nuriwan*
Lacquerware Soup Bowl

「漆器」の一つで、汁物を入れる椀のこと（12頁）。漆器は、ウルシの樹液を木地の器に何度も塗り重ねてつくられる、日本古来のもの。「ジャパン」の英名を持つ。

Lacquerware is made by coating wooden tableware with lacquer sap repeatedly. It is a traditional craft of Japan, and is also known as "Japan."

八寸・*hassun*
Wooden Square Tray

約24cm四方の木地の器。日本では昔、約3cmを一寸といったので、これを八寸という。茶道の食事「懐石」では、これに海の幸と山の幸などの酒肴(しゅこう)を盛り付ける。

A wooden square tray about 24 square cm. *Sun* (寸) is an old Japanese unit for measurement, and one *sun* equals to about 3 cm. The kanji 八 is the number eight. In *kaiseki* in the tea ceremony, food from the sea and the mountains are served in this tray.

曲げわっぱ・*magewappa*
Wooden *Bento* Box

薄くそいだ木の板を曲げて円筒形にした器。高級品は、吸湿性・芳香・殺菌効果を備えたスギを用いて、桜の樹皮で綴じる。弁当箱として使うのが一般的。

Thinly shaved sheets of wood are bent to form a ring to make this container. Cedar is used for expensive ones since it absorbs moisture, has a nice scent and keeps away bacteria. The cedar sheets are then fastened with cherry blossom bark. Used mainly as *bento* boxes.

飯櫃・*meshibitsu*
おひつ・*ohitsu*
Wooden Container for Cooked Rice

ご飯を入れておく木地の器。保温性に優れ、ほどよく米の水分を吸うため、かつては炊き上がったご飯を飯櫃に移してから、ご飯茶碗によそっていた。

A wooden container used to keep cooked rice. Since these containers retain heat and absorb moisture, in the old days, cooked rice was kept in a *meshibitsu* before serving in rice bowls.

燗鍋・*kan-nabe*
Iron Pot for Sake

主に茶道の食事「懐石」で使われる、注ぎ口と手がついた鉄製の酒器。昔は酒を入れた燗鍋を直接火にかけていたが、現在では温めた酒を入れて使う。

Mainly used in *kaiseki* cuisine. In the old days, *kan-nabe* with sake was held over the fire. These days, pre-heated sake is poured into it.

1
朱杯・*shuhai*
Vermillion-lacquered Cups

正式な祝い事や、茶道の食事「懐石」で用いられる朱塗りの杯。燗鍋とセットで供される。

Used for formal celebrations and in *kaiseki* cuisine. Used together with a *kan-nabe*.

2
杯台・*haidai* (*sakazukidai*)
Tray for Vermillion-lacquered Cups

杯を重ねてのせる台。中央に、杯に打った露や残った酒などを入れるための「したみ受け」という穴がある。ただし現在は、したみ受けがこの用途で使われることはない。

Used for stacking up the cups. There is a for pouring in leftover sake, though it is no longer used for this purpose.

___1___
徳利・*tokkuri* (*tokuri*)／銚子・*choshi*
Sake Pitcher

猪口（ちょこ・109頁）に酒を注ぐための、口のすぼんだ器。酒を入れ、徳利ごと燗をする（湯につけて温める）。

A type of flask for pouring sake into a *choko* (page 109). Sake is heated by pouring it into a *tokkuri*, then putting the *tokkuri* in hot water.

___2___
徳利袴・*tokkuri-bakama*
銚子袴・*choshi-bakama*
Holder for *Tokkuri* or *Choshi*

燗をした徳利をのせて、水気や熱を受ける器。漆器が多い。

A kind of tray used to hold *tokkuri* or *choshi* when it is wet and hot. Mostly lacquer.

猪口・*choko* ／杯・*sakazuki*
Sake Cup

酒を注いで飲む器。猪口は昔、小鉢の名前だったが、酒器に転用された後、酒専用につくられるようになった。徳利（108頁）とペアになった磁器製が多い。

Used for drinking sake. *Choko* used to refer to a variety of small bowls, but today the name is used solely for sake cups. Most are *jiki* (porcelain), and come in pairs with *tokkuri* (page 108).

ぐい呑み・*guinomi*
Large Sake Cup

猪口よりも大ぶりの酒を飲む器。「ぐいぐい呑む」もしくは「ぐいっと呑む」という意味から生まれた比較的新しい名前。陶器製のものが多い。

Used for drinking sake, larger in size than a *choko*. Most are *toki* (ceramics).

茶の道具

茶(抹茶以外)を淹れるときに使う道具を紹介する。

1
急須・*kyusu*
Teapot

茶葉を入れ、湯を注いで茶を抽出し、茶碗につぎ分けるための道具。注ぎ口と取っ手がついている。大きさや形はさまざまある。絵は朱泥(しゅでい)の急須(100頁)。

A teapot for making tea, by putting tea leaves and hot water. They come in various shapes and sizes. The picture here shows a *shudei kyusu* (red clay teapot; page 100).

2
茶碗・*chawan* / 湯呑み・*yunomi*
Teacup

煎茶を注いで飲むための磁器製もしくは陶器製の器。

A teacup for drinking tea. The cups come in porcelain or ceramic.

Tea (*cha*) Utensils

Here are some utensils used for serving tea (except powdered green tea).

3

茶托・*chataku*／托子・*takusu*
Saucer for Teacup

茶碗をのせる受け皿。漆器が多い。主に、客に茶を勧めるときに使う。

A saucer on which a *chawan* is placed. Most are lacquer. Generally used when serving tea to a guest.

4

茶筒・*chazutsu*
Container for Tea Leaves

茶葉を保存しておく筒型の容器。漆器製や金属製のものがある。日本の茶筒は密閉度が高く、茶葉の風味をしっかり守ってくれる。

A cylinder-shaped container for preserving tea leaves. They come in lacquerware or metal. Japanese *chazutsu* are airtight and preserve the taste of the tea leaves very well.

5

茶匙・*chasaji*／茶箕・*chami* (*chaki*)
Spoon for Tea Leaves

茶筒から茶葉をすくうための道具。絵のものは、農具の箕に似た形なので、「茶箕」という。漆器製や金属製のものがある。

A kind of spoon used for putting tea leaves into a pot from a *chazutsu*. From its shape which resembles a *mi* (winnowing basket), it is called *chami* ("*cha*" means "tea"). They come in lacquerware or metal.

6

湯冷まし・*yuzamashi*
Cup for Cooling Hot Water

その名の通り、湯を冷ますための器。煎茶(88頁)は約80度の湯で淹れるのが最適といわれ、熱湯をこれに入れて、少し冷ましてから急須に注ぐ。

Used for cooling hot water. *Sencha* (page 88) is said to be best when made with hot water at around 80℃, so hot water is cooled in this *yuzamashi* before pouring it into a teapot.

抹茶の道具

茶道で抹茶（88頁）を点てるときには多くの道具を必要とする。ここでは最小限の道具を紹介する。

抹茶茶碗・*matcha-jawan*
Tea Bowl

抹茶を飲むための器。この器のなかに抹茶を入れて湯を注ぎ、茶筅（113頁）を振って茶をかき混ぜる。煎茶の茶碗（110頁）よりも大ぶりになる。

Used for drinking *matcha*. *Matcha* is put in this bowl and hot water is poured in, which is then blended with a *chasen* (page 113). This bowl is larger than the *chawan* for *sencha* (page 110).

薄茶器・*usuchaki*／棗・*natsume*
Container for Powdered Green Tea

抹茶を入れておく容器。ここから茶杓（113頁）で茶をすくう。さまざまな形や大きさのものがあるが、絵は最も一般的な形。ナツメの実に似ているので「棗（なつめ）」と呼ばれ、薄茶器の代名詞になっている。

A special container for *matcha*. *Matcha* is scooped out of this with a *chashaku* (page 113). Although they come in various shapes and sizes, the one shown here is the most popular shape. Also known as *natsume* (jujube) since it resembles a jujube.

Powdered Green Tea (*matcha*) Utensils

Various utensils are necessary for preparing *matcha* (powdered green tea; page 88) in a tea ceremony. Here we will introduce the minimum utensils needed.

茶筅・*chasen*
Tea Whisk

抹茶と湯をかき混ぜるための道具。竹を80〜100本ほどに細かく割いてつくる。茶筅で抹茶を攪拌（かくはん）することを「茶を点（た）てる」という。

A whisk for blending *matcha* with hot water. Made by splitting bamboo shoots into 80 to 100 extremely thin rods.

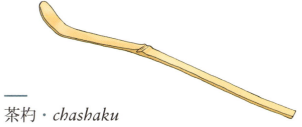

茶杓・*chashaku*
Tea Scoop

抹茶をすくう匙。竹製が一般的だが、象牙や木製などもある。通常、茶杓は専用の筒に入れて保管する。

A spoon for scooping *matcha*. Commonly made of bamboo, though some are made of ivory or wood. A *chashaku* is usually kept in a cylinder-shaped container.

調理器具

日本で古くから親しまれている調理器具を紹介する。

柳刃・*yanagiba*
正夫・*shobu*
Sashimi Knife

魚を刺身に引くときに使う。柳の葉や菖蒲（しょうぶ）の葉のように細身であることから付いた名前。刃渡りは約24cmが標準。

Used for slicing sashimi. Narrow like the leaves of willows and iris, which gave this knife its name. "*Yanagi*" means "willow" and "*ba*" means "blade." The length of its blade is around 24 cm in general.

出刃・*deba*
Cleaver

魚や鶏肉の身をおろすときに使う。刃が厚く、重みもあって骨まで切れる。刃渡りは約15cmが標準。

Used for cutting fish or chicken. With its thick and heavy blade, bones can be cut. The length of its blade is around 15 cm in general.

菜切・*nakiri*
Vegetables Knife

野菜を切るときによく使われる、刃の四角い包丁。「あご」と呼ばれる切っ先の反対側の角が、丸いものは関東型、角ばったものは関西型。

Often used for cutting vegetables. A knife with a square-shaped blade.

Kitchen Utensils and Cookware

Here are some kitchen utensils and cookware that have been used in Japan for a long time.

擂り鉢と擂り粉木・*suribachi and surikogi*
Mortar and Pestle for Grinding

擂り鉢は、内側全体に刻み目のある重い鉢。胡麻や豆腐などの食材を入れ、擂り粉木を使って食材をすりつぶす。「お金をする（失くす）」につながる「する」という言葉を嫌って、「当たり」と言い換えることもある。

A *suribachi* is a heavy mortar with jagged grooves on the inside. Food such as sesame seeds or tofu is put in this mortar and grinded with a *surikogi* (pestle).

胡麻煎り・*gomairi*
Sesame Seeds Roster

網蓋がついた手付きの小鍋。胡麻を入れて火にかけ、こうばしい「煎り胡麻」をつくるのに使うが、豆やぎんなんを煎るときにも便利。

A small pan with a handle and a mesh lid. Sesame seeds are put in for roasting. Also handy when roasting beans or gingko nuts.

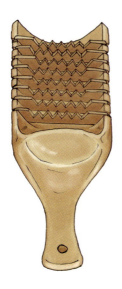

鬼おろし・*oni-oroshi*

Bamboo Grater for Daikon Radish

「おろし」とは、野菜や果物をすりおろすための器具のこと。大根おろしが一般的だが、大根を荒くすりおろすための専用器具に「鬼おろし」がある。

An *oroshi* is a utensil used for grating vegetables and fruit. The most popular vegetable for grating is daikon radish, and there is a special *oroshi* for grating the radish coarsely, which is called *oni* (Japanese mythical ogres)-*oroshi*.

鮫皮おろし・*samekawa-oroshi*

Sharkskin Grater for Wasabi

鮫の皮を貼った、山葵（わさび・66頁）をすりおろすための器具。目の細かい鮫皮ですると、なめらかで、香りと辛みがたった山葵になる。

A grater with *samekawa* (sharkskin), used for grating wasabi (page 66). When fine sharkskin is used, the wasabi becomes smoother with a rich and sharp, spicy fragrance.

杓文字・*shamoji*
Rice Scoop

ご飯をよそうもの。「杓子（しゃくし）」と呼ばれていたが、宮中に使えた女性が、語尾に「もじ」をつけたことから、「杓文字」というようになった。弁財天が持つ琵琶をかたどった形とされる。

Used for serving rice. Though it was originally called *shakushi*, it came to be known as *shamoji* because women working in the courts used the word "*moji*" as a suffix. It is said to be shaped like the *biwa* (Japanese wooden lute) of the *Benzaiten* (Japanese Buddhist goddess).

玉杓子・*tamajakushi*
おたま・*otama*
Wooden Ladle

汁をすくうための道具。「おたま」は略称。カエルの幼生「オタマジャクシ」は玉杓子が語源となっている。

A ladle for serving soup. *Otama* is its abbreviated name. Tadpoles are called *otamajakushi* in Japanese, which derives from *tamajakushi*.

雪平鍋（行平鍋）· *yukihira-nabe*
Yukihira Pan

2つの注ぎ口がついた片手鍋。歌人・在原行平（818〜893）が海女（あま）に塩を焼かせた故事から名前が付いたとされる。本来は銅製や陶製であったが、現在はアルミ製のものが多い。

A single-handled saucepan. Named after a historical event related to the poet Ariwara Yukirihira (818 to 893). Originally made of copper or ceramic. Today, many are made of aluminum.

落とし蓋 · *otoshibuta*
Drop Lid

鍋の中にすっぽり落ち込むサイズの木蓋。煮物をつくるときに落とし蓋を使うと、食材が煮崩れしにくく、味が均一に染みやすくなる。

A wooden lid that fits inside a pot. When an *otoshibuta* is used for making simmered dishes, the ingredients are less likely to fall apart and the lid also works to let the flavor sink in evenly.

卵焼き器・*tamagoyaki-ki*
Square Frying Pan

だし巻玉子や玉子焼（27頁）をつくるための器具。一般的には縦長の長方形だが（関西型）、正方形もある（関東型）。卵汁を卵焼き器に流し込んで巻く作業を何度もくりかえして、焼き上げる。

Used for making *dashimaki-tamago* and *tamago-yaki* (page 27). Typically rectangular-shaped (Kansai-style) but some are square-shaped (Kanto-style). Beaten and flavored eggs are poured in the pan and rolled up several times.

親子鍋・*oyako-nabe*
Donburi Pan

親子丼（28頁）など丼ものの具材を、丼1つ分ずつ調理する器具。柄が上向きについていて、丼のご飯の上にするりと移しやすいのが特徴。

A pan for making single-serving dishes served in bowls on top of rice, such as *oyako-donburi* (page 28). The handle is attached facing upwards, making it easier to slide the contents into the rice in the bowl.

箸

日本の食卓に欠かせない箸。形や素材などさまざまだが、TPOに合わせて使い分けている。

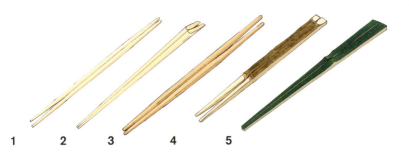

1　2　3　4　5

1
柳箸・*yanagi-bashi* ／祝い箸・*iwai-bashi*
Willow Chopsticks

正月の祝い膳（126頁）や、祝儀の席で用いられる柳製の箸。柳は新春まっさきに芽吹く「芽出たい（めでたい）」木とされている。神様とともに食事をするという気持ちで両端を細くする（一方が神様用、もう一方が人間用）。

Chopsticks made of willow, used for the New Year's celebrations (page 126) and other celebratory occasions. Both ends of these chopsticks are made thin, symbolizing sharing meals with the gods. (One end is for the gods and the other for humans.)

2
盛箸・*mori-bashi*
Chopsticks for Dishing up Food

料理の盛り付けに使う箸。箸先が極細に削られているため、細かい盛り付けがしやすい。金属製のものもある。

The ends are made extremely thin, making it easier to pick up small foods. Some are made of metal.

Chopsticks (*hashi*)

Chopsticks are indispensable in Japanese cuisine. They come in various shapes and are made from different materials. Different chopsticks are used according to TPO.

3

利休箸・*rikyu-bashi*
Rikyu-bashi

両端を細く削って面取りをした箸。茶道を大成した千利休（1522〜1591）が考案したとされ、主に茶道の「懐石」で使われる。赤杉製が正式。

Both ends of these chopsticks are made thin then tapered. It is said the tea master Sen Rikyu (1522 to 1591) invented these chopsticks. Mainly used in *kaiseki* cuisine in the tea ceremony. Ones made of red cedar are used in formal occasions.

4

黒文字・*kuromoji*
Sweet Pick

クロモジという木の皮を一部残して削った菓子用の箸。主に茶道で使われる。菓子を盛った器に添えて取り箸として使うものと、菓子を切る楊枝として1本で使う小さなものとがある。

Made from spicewood, with some bark remaining. Used for sweets, mainly in tea ceremonies. Some *kuromoji* are used to pick up sweets, while smaller ones are used as picks to cut the confectionery into bite-sized pieces.

5

青竹の箸・*aotake no hashi*
Green Bamboo Chopsticks

青竹を削ってつくる箸。主に茶道の料理「懐石」で、取り箸として使われる。竹の節が真ん中にある「中節（なかぶし）」、天（箸先の反対側）にある「天節（てんぶし）」、両端を細くした「両細（りょうぼそ）」の三種類がある。

Chopsticks made of green bamboo. Mainly used as chopsticks to pick up food from serving dishes in *kaiseki* cuisine in the tea ceremony. If a bamboo node is in the middle of the chopstick, they are called *naka-bushi* ("*naka*" means "middle" and "*bushi*" means "node"). When the node is at the end, where one holds the chopsticks, they are called *ten-bushi* ("*ten*" means "top"). When both ends are tapered, they are called *ryoboso* (meaning thin ends).

嫌い箸
Chopstick Taboos

日本の食事に欠かせない箸の扱いのなかに、してはいけない不作法な扱い方があり、「嫌い箸」もしくは「忌み箸」「禁じ箸」と呼ぶ。ここでは代表的な嫌い箸を紹介する。

Chopsticks (*hashi* or *bashi*, depending on the previous word) are an essential item for Japanese cuisine. Here are some of the taboos for when eating with chopsticks.

寄せ箸・*yose-bashi*

箸で食器を引き寄せる。
Dragging a plate towards you with your chopsticks.

涙箸・*namida-bashi*

食材を箸で持ち上げたときに、箸の先から汁をポタポタと落とす。
Picking up food with your chopsticks and letting soup drop from its ends.

刺し箸・*sashi-bashi*

食べ物を箸に突き刺して食べる。
Impaling food with your chopsticks when eating.

探り箸・*saguri-bashi*

料理の中身を探るようにして、箸でかき混ぜる。
Stirring or mixing your food with your chopsticks, as if looking for a certain ingredient.

迷い箸・*mayoi-bashi*

どの料理から食べようかと迷って、箸を宙であちこち動かす。
Moving your chopsticks this way and that way in midair, trying to decide what to eat.

ねぶり箸・*neburi-bashi*

箸についたものを舐（な）めとる。
Licking food off your chopsticks.

箸渡し・*hashi-watashi*

箸で挟んだ食べ物を、他人の箸へ受け渡す。
Passing food from chopsticks to chopsticks.

年中行事

ANNUAL EVENTS

正月（1月）

1年の始まりの月という意味で1月を「正月」ともいう。常の仕事を休んで、各家に歳神様（としがみさま）を迎え、1年の幸運と健康を祈る。

門松・*kadomatsu*

Pine Branch Decoration

家々の門（もん＝かど）に立てる松の飾り。枯れることがない常緑の松は生命力や繁栄を象徴し、歳神はその松に降りて来るという。門松の形は地方によって異なる。

Pine (*matsu*) branch decorations that are put up at the gate (*kado*) of a house. Evergreen pine trees symbolize life force and prosperity, and it is said that they become a dwelling place for the Toshigami-sama. *Kadomatsu* come in different shapes in each region.

鏡餅・*kagami-mochi*

Round Rice Cake Offered to Gods

三方（さんぽう）という台の上に、丸餅と橙（だいだい）、裏白などを飾ったもの。神事の鏡と丸い餅が似ていることからのネーミング。歳神にお供えした餅は、1月11日に下げて家族一緒にいただく。これを「鏡開き」という。

Two or three round *mochi* (rice cakes) put on a wooden offering stand called *sanpo*, together with other decorations such as a *daidai* (bitter orange) and *urajiro* (fern with white-backed leaves). These *mochi* offered to the Toshigami-sama are enjoyed by the entire family on January 11th.

New Year (January)

People take leave from work to welcome Toshigami-sama (the Shinto deity of the incoming new year) and wish for good fortune and health.

関西型
Kansai-style

関東型
Kanto-style

伊勢型
Ise-style

注連飾り・*shime-kazari*
Straw Festoon Decoration

稲藁でつくった注連縄に、裏白や橙などの縁起物をつけたもの。本来、注連縄は神様のいる聖域と俗界との境を示すもので、神社でよく見かける。正月は家の玄関に飾って、神様がなかにいることを示す。

Straw *shimenawa* (festoons) decorated with good-luck charms such as *urajiro* and *daidai*. *Shimenawa* is the border between the sacred place and the secular quarter, and is often seen in shrines. For the New Year, they are hung at the entrance of a house to indicate that the Gods are inside.

祝い肴三種・*iwai-zakana sanshu*
三つ肴・*mitsu-zakana*
Three Good-luck Foods

一般に、黒豆・数の子（ニシンの卵巣）・ごまめ（干したカタクチイワシ）を指す。黒豆の「まめ」は健康を意味する言葉、ニシンの卵は子孫繁栄を表す。田んぼの肥料にしていたため「田作り」の別名もあるごまめは、五穀豊穣に通じる。この3つを食して、1年の健康・子孫繁栄・五穀豊穣を祈る。

Commonly indicate *kuromame* (black beans), *kazunoko* (herring roe) and *gomame* (small dried sardines). They are eaten to wish for good health, prosperity of descendants and good harvest throughout the year.

御節料理・*osechi-ryori* ／ 祝い重・*iwaiju*
Traditional Dishes for the New Year

祝い肴や鯛・海老・くわいなど縁起のよい食材を使った、正月の料理を「御節料理」と呼ぶ。「めでたさを重ねる」という意味で重箱（じゅうばこ）に入れる。本来、五節句の際に神様にお供えして、家族もいただく料理を「御節供（ごせっく）料理」といった。

A traditional meal for the New Year with food that brings good luck, such as *iwai-zakana*, sea bream, prawn and arrowhead bulbs. They are all packed together in a tiered lacquer box called *jubako*, which indicates multilayered auspiciousness.

雑煮 • *zoni*
Soup Containing Rice Cakes

正月に食べる、餅をメインにした汁物。本来は歳神にお供えしたいろいろな食材を煮たものだった。餅の形、食材、汁の種類は地方によって特色がある。

A special *mochi* (rice cake) soup for the New Year. The ingredients and type of soup are different in each region.

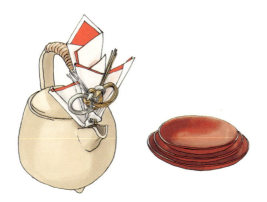

屠蘇酒 • *tososhu*
New Year's Spiced Sake

屠蘇散（山椒、桔梗の根、肉桂などの生薬を配合したもの）を日本酒やみりんに浸した薬酒。長寿を願っていただく。年少者から順に飲む習いもあり、若い気を年長者に分ける意味がある。

A special sake made by putting *tososan* (a bag containing a mixture of spices such as *sansho* pepper, root of Chinese bellflower and cinnamon) into sake or *mirin*. Sipped to wish for longevity.

人日の節句（1月7日）

日本には、季節の変わり目に無病息災と家内安全を祈る行事（節句）がある。人日、上巳（3月3日）、端午（5月5日）、七夕（7月7日）、重陽（9月9日）の5つを「五節句（ごせっく）」という。

七草粥・*nanakusagayu*

Rice Porridge Containing Seven Kinds of Spring Herbs

7種類の若菜を入れた粥。1年の無病息災を祈るため、人日（じんじつ）の節句に食べる。7種は地方によって異なるが、右頁の七草を入れるところが多い。昔は6日の夜もしくは7日の早朝に、七草を俎板（まないた）の上にのせ、言葉をはやしながら包丁で刻んだ。これを「七草叩き」という。

A seven-herb rice porridge eaten for the Festival of Seven Herbs to wish for good health. Although the herbs used for this porridge vary according to different regions, the seven herbs on the right are most common.

Festival of Seven Herbs (January 7th)

The festival on January 7th is *jinjitsu no sekku*. Seasonal festivals in which people wish for good health and safety of the family are called *sekku*.

せり Water Dropwort

なずな Shepherd's Purse

ごぎょう Jersey Cudweed

はこべら Common Chickweed

ほとけのざ Nipplewort

すずな Turnip

すずしろ Japanese Daikon Radish

節分（2月3日頃）

節分とは本来、季節の変わり目「立春・立夏・立秋・立冬」の前日をいうが、現在は立春の前日を「節分」と称して厄払いをする。

豆まき・*mamemaki*
追儺・*tsuina* ／ 鬼やらい・*oni-yarai*
Scattering Soybeans

「鬼は外」「福は内」と唱えながら、家の各所に豆をまき、災いの象徴・鬼を追い払う行事。本来は事前に枡に盛って、神様にお供えした「福豆」を使う。まき終えたら、自分の年の数だけ豆を食べて息災を願う。

An event to drive away *oni*, which symbolizes misfortune, by scattering roasted soybeans outside and inside the home, shouting "Devil out!" and "Happiness in!" Afterwards, people eat their ages' worth of beans to wish for good health.

恵方巻き・*eho-maki*
Futo-maki for Setsubun

節分の日に食べて商売繁盛や無病息災を祈る太巻き寿司（57頁）。その年の恵方（歳徳神が居る方角）を向いて、願い事をしながら、黙ったまま一本を食べつくす。近年、全国的に広がっている。

Futo-maki (page 57) eaten on *Setsubun* to wish for thriving business and good health. This custom of enjoying *eho-maki* has spread all over the country in recent years.

Setsubun (Around February 3rd)

Setsubun originally refers to the day before the calendarial beginning of spring, summer, autumn and winter. Today, the day before the beginning of spring is called *Setsubun* and it is a day to drive away mishap.

柊鰯・*hiiragi-iwashi*
Decoration for Keeping Away *Oni*

焼いた鰯の頭を、柊の小枝に刺したもの。これを家の戸口に飾ると、鰯の強い臭いと柊の葉の棘を嫌って、鬼（災い）が入ってこないとされる。

The head of grilled sardines (*iwashi*) on a twig of Japanese holly (*hiiragi*). By hanging this at the entrance of a house, the strong smell of sardines and prickles of the Japanese holly are said to keep away *oni*.

上巳の節句／桃の節句／雛祭り（3月3日）

雛人形を飾ったり、縁起物を食べたりして、女の子の成長を願う行事。人形（ひとがた）を川に流して心身を祓い清める風習や、貴族の娘の人形遊びなどが合流して、現在のかたちになった。

蛤のお吸い物・*hamaguri no osuimono*
Clams in Clear Soup

春の食材・蛤を使った澄まし汁。2枚の貝殻のように、一生添い遂げる夫と出会えることを願っていただく。

Clear soup cooked with clams, which is a seasonal food of spring. This is enjoyed in hopes of a girl meeting her perfect match and living happily ever after.

菱餅・*hishi-mochi*
Lozenge-shaped Rice Cake

桃色・白・緑の餅を菱形にして重ねたもの。菱は子孫繁栄を象徴する。白は雪で清浄を、桃色は桃の花で魔除けを、緑は新緑で健康を表す。

Three-tiered lozenge-shaped rice cakes in pink, white and green. The white represents snow, meaning purity, the pink represents peach blossoms for warding off evil spirits and the green represents fresh verdure to indicate good health.

ひなあられ・*hina-arare*
Cubic Rice Crackers for the Girl's Doll Festival

米もしくは豆を炒って、桃色・白・緑などに着色し、砂糖をまぶしたお菓子。関西では醤油味や塩味のあられが一般的。

A confectionery made by roasting rice or beans, then coating them with pink, white or green-colored sugar.

Girls' Doll Festival (March 3rd)

An event to wish for the healthy growth of girls by setting up *hina* dolls and eating good-luck food.

1
犬筥・*inubako*／御伽犬・*otogi-inu*
Lidded Ornaments of Pair Dogs

雌雄一対の犬の蓋物。安産かつ多産とされる犬にあやかって、雛人形などといっしょに飾る。女の子の幸せを祈る嫁入り道具の一つでもあった。

Lidded ornaments of dogs that come in male-female pairs. Since dogs have many puppies and safe delivery, these ornaments are displayed together with *hina* dolls.

2
雪洞・*bombori*
Classic Candlestand

絹や紙を張った覆いのある、昔の蠟燭（ろうそく）立て。ものが透けてぼんやり見えることからのネーミング。雛人形といっしょに飾る。

A small lampstand covered with silk or paper lampshade which held candles in the old days. Displayed together with *hina* dolls.

端午の節句／こどもの日（5月5日）

兜などの武具を飾ったり、お菓子を食べたりして、男の子の成長を祝う行事。菖蒲や蓬を飾って穢れを祓うのが本来のならわし。菖蒲と「尚武」の語呂合わせから、男の子の行事となった。

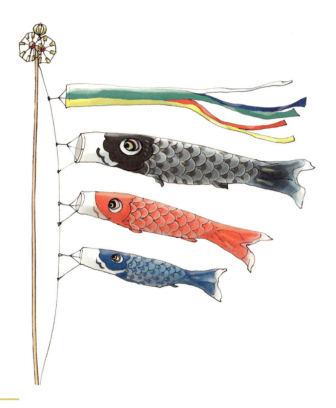

鯉のぼり・*koi-nobori*
Carp-shaped Streamers

鯉を模した布や紙をつけたのぼり旗。急流の滝を登った鯉が龍になったという故事「龍門（りゅうもん）」から、鯉は立身出世の象徴とされる。のぼりの天辺にある5色の「吹流し」は、鯉を守る厄除けとなっている。

Carp-shaped streamers made from fabric or paper. Carp is said to symbolize success. The five-colored tubular streamer at the very top of the *koi-nobori* is called *fukinagashi*, and is for protecting the carps from evil spirits.

Boy's Festival (May 5th)

An event to wish for the healthy growth of boys by setting up armor such as a *kabuto* (warrior's helmet) and eating traditional sweets.

粽・*chimaki*
Rice Dumpling Wrapped in a Bamboo Leaf

餅や葛生地などを笹の葉でくるんで蒸した菓子。笹の葉に包んだご飯は、戦場へ行く武士の携帯食だったことから、端午の節句菓子になった。

Mochi (rice cake) or kudzu dough wrapped in a bamboo leaf and steamed. Rice wrapped in bamboo leaves used to be carried by samurai as portable food, which is why *chimaki* became a signature confectionery for this festival.

柏餅・*kashiwa-mochi*
Rice Cake Stuffed with Sweet Bean Paste and Wrapped in an Oak Leaf

餡入りの餅を柏の葉1枚ではさんだ菓子。柏は神聖な木とされ、新葉が出るまで古い葉が落ちないことから、親が子の無事を見届けられるようにという願いを託して食べる。

Mochi with sweet red bean paste wrapped in an oak (*kashiwa*) leaf. The oak is said to be a sacred tree. Since the leaves stay on the tree until a new leaf sprouts, this confectionery is eaten in hope that parents may live to see their children grow happily through adulthood.

夏越しの祓（6月30日）

日本には、半年間で溜まった穢れを清める行事が1年に2度ある。大晦日の「大祓（おおはらえ）」と、ここで紹介する「夏越しの祓」である。

茅の輪くぐり・*chinowa kuguri*

Chigaya Ring Passing

茅草（かやぐさ）でつくった大きな輪を神社の境内に立て、それをくぐることで穢れを祓う行事。くぐり方に作法があり、参詣者は8の字を描くように茅の輪をくぐる。紙でつくった形代（かたしろ）を川に流して「夏越しの祓」とする神社もある。

A purification ceremony conducted by passing through a *chinowa*, a large ring made of thatch, set up in the precincts of a shrine. Visitors go through the ring several times as if drawing the number eight with their steps.

Summer Passage Ritual (June 30th)

Japan has two rituals a year for purifying the past six-month's *kegare* (impurity). One is called *Nagoshi no Harae* and the other is *Oharae* on the New Year's Eve.

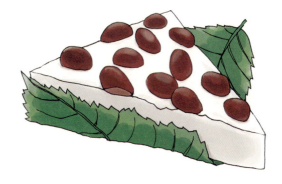

水無月・*minazuki*
Triangle-shaped Rice Jelly

三角形の外郎（ういろう）に小豆を散らした菓子。夏越しの祓に無病息災を願って食べるが、小豆は厄除け、三角形は氷を表し、暑気払いの意味もある。かつて宮中では旧暦6月1日に氷を食べる風習があり、庶民がそれにならって氷を模した菓子をつくったのが始まりといわれる。

A triangle-shaped *uiro* (sweet steamed rice jelly) topped with adzuki beans. Eaten for the Summer Passage Ritual to wish for good health. The adzuki beans ward off evil spirits and the triangular shape represents ice, which is for driving away the summer heat.

七夕（7月7日）

7月7日にだけ逢瀬を許される織姫と彦星の伝説にちなむ節句。裁縫や技芸の上達を願う古代中国の行事と、布を織って先祖を迎える日本の「棚機（たなばた）」の行事が習合したものといわれる。

笹飾り・*sasa-kazari*

Bamboos Decorations

願い事を書いた短冊を、笹竹に結ぶ風習。まっすぐ伸びる竹にのって、短冊の願い事が天に届くようにという意味がある。昔は、芋の葉におりた露で墨をすって、梶の葉に願い事を書いた。

A tradition of tying *tanzaku*, narrow strips of paper inscribed with wishes, on leafed bamboo branches. Since bamboo grows long and straight, people hope that their wishes will reach heaven together with the bamboo.

Tanabata Festival/Star Festival (July 7th)

A festival based on the legend of *Orihime* (Vega) and *Hikoboshi* (Altair), the two stars which are allowed to meet only once a year on July 7th.

素麺 • *somen*
Fine Wheat Noodles

七夕には冷たい素麺を食べて暑さをしのぐ。古代中国で、熱病除けに索餅（さくべい）という菓子（素麺の元祖とされる）を食べる風習が伝わったともいわれる。

Cold *somen* are enjoyed on *Tanabata* to bear the summer heat.

願いの糸 • *negai no ito*
五色の麻苧 • *goshiki no asao*
Five-colored Threads

七夕に飾る5色の糸。青、赤、黄、白、黒の5色は中国の五行（ごぎょう）説（宇宙を五つのものにあてはめて考える思想）が基になっている。糸は裁縫の上達を願った時代のなごり。

Used for decoration on *Tanabata*. They are based on a Chinese theory in which nature is believed to be made up of five elements that are represented by five colors: blue, red, yellow, white and black. The threads represented women's hopes for improvement in their needlework skills.

お盆／盂蘭盆会（うらぼんえ・旧暦7月15日前後）

先祖の霊を迎えて供養する仏教の行事。旧暦7月15日前後の行事だが、新暦にあてはめて8月に行う地域が多い。日本の社会には「お盆休み」という休暇がある。

迎え火・*mukaebi*

Fire to Welcome the Souls of Ancestors

先祖の霊は13日の夕方に迎え、14日と15日をともに過ごし、16日に見送る。13日は苧殻（おがら・麻の茎を干したもの）を燃やして「迎え火」とし、16日の夕方に「送り火」を焚いて帰路をてらす。京都の「大文字」はこの送り火を大規模にした行事である。

The souls of ancestors are welcomed in the evening of July 13th on the lunar calendar. People spend time with them on the 14th and the 15th, then send the souls back on the 16th. *Ogara* (dried hemp stems) are burnt to welcome the souls on the 13th, and to light up their way back on the 16th. The Daimonji in Kyoto is a bonfire event for this send-off.

Bon Festival/Lantern Festival (Middle of July on the Lunar Calendar)

A Buddhist festival to welcome and console the souls of ancestors. There is a short vacation called *obon-yasumi* (Bon vacation) in Japan.

精霊馬 ・ *shoryo-uma*
Cucumber Horses for the Souls of Ancestors

きゅうりを馬に、茄子を牛に見立てた夏野菜のお供えもの。4つの足は芋殻でつくる。先祖の霊は馬に乗り、牛に荷物を載せてくるといわれる。

Offerings likening cucumbers to horses and eggplants to cows. It is said that the souls of ancestors ride on these horses with their belongings carried by the cows.

精進料理 ・ *shojin-ryori*
Vegetarian Dish

植物性の食材だけを使った料理。ダシも鰹節ではなく昆布などを用いる。お盆期間は、先祖の霊をもてなすために精進料理を供える。

During the *Bon Festival*, *shojin-ryori* is prepared to entertain the souls of our ancestors.

十五夜の月見・中秋の名月・芋名月（旧暦8月15日）

月の満ち欠けに基づく旧暦では15日の月は必ず満月になり、「十五夜の月」という。この時期の「十五夜の月」は、空気が澄んでいるので特に美しく、月を愛でながら秋の実りに感謝する。

Moon-viewing (August 15th on the Lunar Calendar)

On the lunar calendar, which is based on the cycle of moon phases, the 15th of the month is always a full moon. This is called *jugoya no tsuki* (the moon of the 15th). The 15th of August (on the lunar calendar) is the time for viewing the full moon and celebrating the autumn harvest.

月見飾り・*tsukimi-kazari*
Decoration for Moon-viewing

月見をする場所には、三方（さんぽう）という台にのせた15個の月見団子と薄（すすき）を供えて、大地の恵みに感謝し、来年の豊作を祈る。月見団子は十五夜の満月を表し、薄の穂は神様がおりてくる依代（よりしろ）となっている。里芋・栗など秋の産物をいっしょに供えることがあるので、「芋名月」ともいう。

Fifteen *tsukimi-dango* (rice-flour dumplings) are set out as offerings, together with *susuki* (Japanese pampas grass). They are for thanking nature's blessing and wishing for next year's good harvest. The 15 dumplings represent the full moon of the 15th, and the Japanese pampas grass is a place for the gods to dwell. Autumn crops such as taro and chestnuts may be offered too, which is why *jugoya no tsuki* is also called *imo* (taro) *meigetsu* (harvest moon).

重陽の節句（9月9日）

不老長寿の象徴である菊にあやかり、長命を祈る行事。中国の陰陽説では奇数が「陽」で9が最大数となり、陽が重なる9月9日は陽の極まる日とされる。

茱萸袋・*gumi-bukuro*
Bag Containing Goumi Berries

薬用の茱萸（ぐみ）の実と菊を入れた赤い袋。身につけたり、家の柱に掛けて、厄除けにする。袋の口に茱萸と菊の花をさした茱萸袋もある。

A red bag containing goumi berries for medicinal use and chrysanthemums. They are attached to the pillars of houses or carried around, to ward off evil spirits. The berries and flowers are sometimes arranged like a bouquet by using the bag as a vase.

菊の被綿・*kiku no kisewata*
Chrysanthemum Silk Floss

9月8日の夜に、菊の花の上に真綿（絹糸）を被せ、夜露と菊の香りをしみ込ませたもの。9日朝にその真綿で体を拭いて美と健康を祈る。

On the night of September 8th, chrysanthemum blossoms (*kiku*) are covered with silk floss to let the evening dew and the scent of the flowers sink in. People rub their bodies with this silk the following morning to wish for beauty and good health.

Chrysanthemum Festival (September 9th)

A festival to wish for longevity, named after the chrysanthemum, which is a symbol of perpetual youth and longevity. This festival is called *choyo no sekku*.

菊酒・*kiku-zake*
Chrysanthemum Sake

菊の花びらを浸した酒。無病息災・不老長寿を願っていただく。平安時代の宮中では、菊を鑑賞し、詩歌を詠みながら菊酒を飲んだという。

Chrysanthemum-infused sake. Enjoyed to wish for good health, perpetual youth and longevity. In the courts during the Heian period (8th to 11th century), it is said that people had this sake while enjoying the view of the chrysanthemums and composing Japanese poems.

栗ご飯・*kuri-gohan*
Chestnut Rice

重陽の節句は栗の節句ともいわれ、旬の栗を混ぜ込んだご飯をいただく。「もってのほか」と呼ばれる食用菊も使われる。

This festival is also known as *Kuri no Sekku* (the festival of chestnuts). Rice cooked with chestnuts, which is a seasonal autumn dish, is enjoyed. Edible chrysanthemums called *mottenohoka* are also used for this dish.

大晦日／大つごもり（12月31日）

12月31日は、新年を迎えるために掃除をしたり、長寿を祈って蕎麦を食べたりする。日付が変わる直前には、お寺で鐘を撞いて煩悩を打ち払い（除夜の鐘）、清らかに新年を迎える。

年越し蕎麦・*toshikoshi-soba*
つごもり蕎麦・*tsugomori-soba*

Soba Noodles Eaten on New Year's Eve

大晦日の夜に食べる蕎麦のこと。その由来には諸説があるが、「細く長い」蕎麦にあやかって、長寿を願って食べる、切れやすい蕎麦にあやかってその年の悪いことを断ち切って新年を迎える、などの説が聞かれる。

Various theories exist behind this custom, the most popular ones are that these long and thin noodles are eaten in hope for longevity, and that since they can be bitten off easily, they signify cutting off all the troubles of the past year.

New Year's Eve

December 31st is the day for cleaning the house for the coming new year, or enjoying *soba* to wish for longevity. Right before the date changes, Buddhist bells are rung out at temples to dispel worldly desires and to welcome a fresh new year.

おけら詣り・*okera-mairi*

Okera-mairi in Kyoto

おけらでつくった縄に、神火（火きり臼と火きり杵で切り出し、神前に捧げた火）をいただいて持ち帰る、京都八坂神社の大晦日の行事。その火を使って、新年の雑煮（127頁）などを調理すると邪気が祓われ、新しい年を無病息災に過ごせるといわれている。

A New Year's Eve festival in Yasaka Shrine in Kyoto in which ropes made from *okera* (Atractylis ovata) are set ablaze. The fire is an offering to the gods. Visitors take embers of this fire back home with the *okera*. It is said that by using this fire to cook *zoni* (page 127), evil spirits will be warded off and the new year will be spent in good health.

索引（五十音順） Index for Japanese

和食
JAPANESE COOKING

あ	青紫蘇	Green Perilla	68
	青芽	Young Buds of Green Perilla	69
	青柚	Green Yuzu Citrus	70
	青柚子	Green Yuzu Citrus	70
	赤貝	Ark Shell	49
	上がり	Green Tea	37
	揚物	Deep-fried Dish	15
	鯵	Horse Mackerel	44
	紫陽花金団	Kinton Likened to the Flowers of the Hydrangea	84
	穴子	Conger Eel	52
	有平糖	Sugar Candy Mixed with Starch Syrup	80
	泡盛	Distilled Liquor Made from Rice	91
	餡蜜	Agar-jelly Cubes with Sweet Bean Paste in Syrup	76
	烏賊	Squid	50
	イクラ軍艦巻き	Salmon Roe Battleship Roll	54
	稲荷寿司	Vinegared Rice Stuffed in a Bag of Abura-age	58
	亥の子餅	Rice Cake Representing the Baby Boar	87
	今川焼き	Pancake Stuffed with Sweet Bean Paste	79
	鰯の煮干し	Dried Sardines	61
	鶯餅	Rice Cake Coated with Green Soybean Flour	82
	うどん	Udon Noodles	30
	鰻の蒲焼	Broiled Eel Flavored with Thick Sweetened Soy Sauce	27
	鰻の白焼	Broiled Eel without Sauce	27

	ウニ軍艦巻き	Sea Urchin Battleship Roll	55
	卯の花	Dish with Tofu Refuse	23
	海老	Prawn	46
	大葉	Green Perilla	68
	大判焼き	Pancake Stuffed with Sweet Bean Paste	79
	おから	Dish with Tofu Refuse	23
	お好み焼き	Japanese Pancake Fried with Various Ingredients	26
	押し寿司	Pressed Sushi	58
	おてしょう	Small Plate for Soy Sauce	37
	落とし文	Confectionery Shaped Like Rolled-up Leaves	84
	おはぎ	Glutinous Rice Ball Coated with Sweet Bean Paste	86
	親子丼	Bowl of Rice Topped with Chicken and Egg	28
か	回転焼き	Pancake Stuffed with Sweet Bean Paste	79
	鰹節	Dried Bonito	60
	かっぱ巻き	Cucumber Roll	56
	蟹みそ軍艦巻き	Crab Butter Battleship Roll	55
	かぼす	Kabosu Citrus	70
	蒲鉾	Steamed Fish Paste Cake	22
	がめ煮	Chikuzen-style Stew	20
	唐揚げ	Deep-fried Food	21
	辛み	Spice	63
	がり	Pickled Ginger	39
	雁が音	Green Tea Made of Stalks	89
	萱草	Hemerocallis Fulva	73
	甘味	Sweets	17
	雁擬き	Deep-fried Tofu Burger	24
	刻み柚子	Kizami-yuzu	71
	きしめん	Flat Wheat Noodles	31
	きつね	Soba or Udon with Abura-age	34
	木の芽	Buds of Japanese Pepper	67
	黄柚子	Yellow Yuzu Citrus	71
	玉	Omelet	39
	玉露	Green Tea of the Highest Quality	88
	金鍔	Baked Sweet Bean Paste Coated with Thin Dough	77
	金目鯛の煮付け	Simmered Alfonsino	18

	茎茶	Green Tea Made of Stalks	89
	草餅	Rice Cake Mixed with Mugwort	83
	葛饅頭	Bun with a Bean Paste Filling Covered with Kudzu Starch	85
	軍艦巻き	Battleship Roll	39
	けん	Shredded Vegetables with Sashimi	63
	玄猪餅	Rice Cake Representing the Baby Boar	87
	玄米茶	Green Tea mixed Roasted Popped Rice	89
	香の物	Pickled Vegetables	16
	木の葉丼	Bowl of Rice Topped with Kamaboko, Vegetables and egg	28
	ご飯	Rice	16
	昆布	Dried Kombu Kelp	60
	金平糖	Sugar Candy	80
さ	先付	First Dish in the Course	12
	桜餅	Rice Cake Wrapped in a Cherry Leaf	83
	刺身	Sashimi	13
	鯖の味噌煮	Mackerel Simmered in Miso Sauce	18
	ざる蕎麦	Cold Soba Noodles Served in a Zaru	33
	秋刀魚	Saury	45
	強肴	Side Dish	15
	蝦蛄	Squilla	47
	しゃぶしゃぶ	Shabu-Shabu	25
	しゃり	White Rice	36
	生姜	Ginger	66
	焼酎	Distilled Spirits	91
	薯蕷饅頭	Bun Stuffed with Sweet Bean Paste	78
	白和え	Tofu Dressing	23
	吸口	Fragrant Garnish Added to Wanmono	65
	吸地	Soup of Wanmono	65
	すき焼き	Sukiyaki	25
	進肴	Side Dish	15
	すだち	Sudachi Citrus	70
	せいろ蕎麦	Cold Soba Noodles Served in a Seiro	33
	善哉	Sweet Red Bean Soup with a Piece of Rice Cake	76
	煎茶	Green Tea	88
	薇	Osmunda	75
	そうめん	Fine Wheat Noodles	30
	蕎麦	Soba Noodles	32
	蕎麦猪口	Dipping Soup Cup for Soba	33

た	鯛	Sea Bream	41
	鯛の兜煮	Simmered Head of Sea Bream	19
	炊き合せ	Assorted Simmered Dish	14
	蛸	Octopus	51
	たこ焼き	Small Ball of Wheat Flour with Bits of Octopus	26
	だし巻き玉子	Omelet	27
	たぬき（大阪）	Soba with Abura-age	34
	たぬき（関東）	Soba or Udon with Tenkasu	34
	タネ	Ingredients of Sushi	36
	玉子	Omelet	39
	玉子焼き	Omelet	27
	たらの芽	Buds of Japanese Angelica	72
	筑前煮	Chikuzen-style Stew	20
	竹輪	Cylindrical Fish Sausage	22
	茶碗蒸し	Egg Custard Steamed in a Cup	29
	中華めん	Chinese Noodles	31
	ちらし寿司（関西）	Scattered Sushi with Seasoned Iingredients	59
	ちらし寿司（関東）	Scattered Sushi with Fresh Ingredients	59
	付出し	First Dish in the Course	12
	月見	Soba or Udon Topped with a Raw Egg	35
	土筆	Spore Shoot of Field Horsetail	74
	造り	Sashimi	13
	つま	Garnish Served with Sashimi	63
	手塩皿	Small Plate for Soy Sauce	37
	鉄火巻き	Tuna Roll	56
	てっさ	Sashimi of Grobefish	53
	手巻き寿司	Hand-rolled Sushi	57
	天ぷら	Tempura	21
	天盛り	Toppings of Dishes	63
	飛び子軍艦巻き	Flying-fish Roe Battleship Roll	54
	土瓶蒸し	Food Cooked in an Earthen Teapot	29
	止椀	Miso Soup	16
	どら焼き	Two Pancakes with Sweet Bean Paste in Between	79
	とろろ	Soba or Udon Topped with Grated Yam	35
な	菜の花	Canola Blossoms	72
	にぎり寿司	Hand-shaped Sushi	38
	日本酒	Sake	90

	煮物	Assorted Simmered Dish	14
	ネタ	Ingredients of Sushi	36
	野蒜	Wild Rocambole	73
は	はいから（関西）	Soba or Udon with Tenkasu	34
	萩の餅	Glutinous Rice Ball Coated with Sweet Bean Paste	86
	花菜	Canola Blossoms	72
	花びら餅	Rice Cake with Burdock and Miso-flavored Sweet Bean Paste	82
	花穂紫蘇	Ear of Shiso Flowers	68
	ばらん	Partition Sheet	37
	番茶	Roasted Green Tea	89
	はんぺん	Fish-cake Made of Fish Paste and Yam	22
	平目のえんがわ	Fluke Fin of Olive Flounder	43
	飛竜頭	Deep-fried Tofu Burger	24
	吹き寄せ	An Assortment of Dried Confectionery Representing the Autumn Season	86
	太巻き	Thick Roll	57
	フライ	Deep-fried Food with Bread Crumbs	21
	鰤	Yellowtail	42
	鰤大根	Yellowtail Simmered with Daikon Radish	19
	へぎ柚子	Hegi-yuzu	71
	焙じ茶	Roasted Green Tea	89
	防風	Glehnia Littoralis	67
	干し椎茸	Dried Shiitake Mushroom	61
	穂紫蘇	Young Spikes of Perilla	68
	細巻き	Thin Roll	39
	帆立	Scallop	48
ま	鮪	Tuna	40
	松風	Baked Cake Made from Sugar and Wheat Flour	81
	抹茶	Powdered Green Tea	88
	松葉柚子	Matuba-yuzu	71
	豆大福	Rice Cake Stuffed with Sweet Bean Paste	78
	三笠	Two Pancakes with Sweet Bean Paste in Between	79
	水（有平糖）	Sugar Candy Representing the Flow of Water	85
	水菓子	Fruits	17

	味噌田楽	Grilled Food Coated with Miso Glaze	24
	茗荷	Japanese Ginger	66
	向付	Sashimi	13
	紫芽	Young Buds of Red Perilla	69
	芽葱	Sprouts of Long Green Onion	67
	最中	Wafers Cakes Stuffed with Sweet Bean Paste	79
や	焼物	Broiled Dish	13
	薬味	Condiment	33
	山独活	Wild Udo	74
	山かけ	Soba or Udon Topped with Grated Yam	35
	雪餅	Snow-white Kinton	87
	湯桶	Sobayu Pot	33
	羊羹	Bar of Jellied Sweet Bean Paste	77
	蓬餅	Rice Cake Mixed with Mugwort	83
ら	落雁	Pressed Cake Made of Rice Flour and Sugar	81
わ	若竹煮	Simmered Bamboo Shoots with Wakame	20
	山葵	Wasabi	66
	蕨	Bracken	75
	椀種	Main Ingredient of Wanmono	65
	椀づま	Seasonal Vegetables with Wandane	65
	椀物	Clear Soup of the Season	12
	椀盛	Clear Soup of the Season	12

食器
TABLEWARE

あ	青竹の箸	Green Bamboo Chopsticks	121
	有田焼	Arita Ware	96
	伊賀焼	Iga Ware	99
	伊万里焼	Imari Ware	96
	色絵	Overglaze Enamels	95
	祝い箸	Willow Chopsticks	120
	伊部焼	Imbe Ware	100
	薄茶器	Container for Powdered Green Tea	112
	おたま	Wooden Ladle	117
	落とし蓋	Drop Lid	118
	鬼おろし	Bamboo Grater for Daikon Radish	116
	おひつ	Wooden Container for Cooked Rice	106
	親子鍋	Donburi Pan	119
	織部焼	Oribe-style Mino Ware	98
か	角皿	Square Plate	102
	片口	Lipped Bowl	104
	唐津焼	Karatsu Ware	101
	燗鍋	Iron Pot for Sake	107
	急須	Teapot	110
	清水焼	Kiyomizu Ware	97
	ぐい呑み	Large Sake Cup	109
	九谷焼	Kutani Ware	97
	黒文字	Sweet Pick	121
	胡麻煎り	Sesame Seeds Roaster	115
さ	杯	Sake Cup	109
	鮫皮おろし	Sharkskin Grater for Wasabi	116
	信楽焼	Shigaraki Ware	99
	志野焼	Shino-style Mino Ware	98
	杓文字	Rice Scoop	117
	朱杯	Vermillion-lacquered Cup	107
	正夫	Sashimi Knife	114
	擂り鉢と擂り粉木	Mortar and Pestle for Grinding	115
	青磁	Blue Porcelain	94
	染付	Blue and White Porcelain	95
た	托子	Saucer for Teacup	111
	卵焼き器	Square Frying Pan	119
	玉杓子	Wooden Ladle	117

	茶匙	Spoon for Tea Leaves	111
	茶杓	Tea Scoop	113
	茶筅	Tea Whisk	113
	茶托	Saucer for Teacup	111
	茶筒	Container for Tea Leaves	111
	茶箕	Spoon for Tea Leaves	111
	茶碗	Teacup	110
	銚子	Sake Pitcher	108
	銚子袴	Holder for Choshi	108
	猪口	Sake Cup	109
	手付鉢	Dish with Handle	104
	出刃	Cleaver	114
	常滑焼	Tokoname Ware	100
	徳利	Sake Pitcher	108
	徳利袴	Holder for Tokkuri	108
な	長皿	Rectangular Plate	102
	菜切	Vegetables Knife	114
	棗	Container for Powdered Tea	112
	なます皿	Namasu Plate	103
	塗椀	Lacquerware Soup Bowl	105
は	杯台	Tray for Vermillion-lacquered Cups	107
	萩焼	Hagi Ware	101
	白磁	White Porcelain	94
	八寸	Wooden Square Tray	106
	備前焼	Bizen Ware	100
ま	曲げわっぱ	Wooden Bento Box	106
	抹茶茶碗	Tea Bowl	112
	俎板皿	Flat Rectangular Plate	102
	向付	Mukozuke Bowl	103
	飯櫃	Wooden Container for Cooked Rice	106
	盛箸	Chopsticks for Dishing up Food	120
や	柳刃	Sashimi Knife	114
	柳箸	Willow Chopsticks	120
	雪平鍋(行平鍋)	Yukihira Pan	118
	湯冷まし	Cup for Cooling Hot Water	111
	湯呑み	Teacup	110
	四方皿	Square Plate	102
ら	利休箸	Rikyu-bashi	121
わ	割山椒	Cup with Three Slits	105

索引(五十音順)

年中行事
ANNUAL EVENTS

あ	犬筥	Lidded Ornaments of Pair Dogs	133
	祝い肴三種	Three Good-luck Foods	126
	祝い重	Traditional Dishes for the New Year	126
	恵方巻き	Futo-maki for Setsubun	130
	おけら詣り	Okera-mairi in Kyoto	147
	御節料理	Traditional Dishes for the New Year	126
	御伽犬	Lidded Ornaments of Pair Dogs	133
	鬼やらい	Scattering Soybeans	130
か	鏡餅	Round Rice Cake Offered to Gods	124
	柏餅	Rice Cake Stuffed with Sweet Bean Paste and Wrapped in an Oak Leaf	135
	門松	Pine Branch Decoration	124
	菊酒	Chrysanthemum Sake	145
	菊の被綿	Chrysanthemum Silk Floss	144
	茱萸袋	Bag Containing Goumi Berries	144
	栗ご飯	Chestnut Rice	145
	鯉のぼり	Carp-shaped Streamers	134
	ごぎょう	Jersey Cudweed	129
	五色の麻苧	Five-colored Threads	139
さ	笹飾り	Bamboos Decorations	138
	注連飾り	Straw Festoon Decoration	125
	精進料理	Vegetarian Dish	141
	精霊馬	Cucumber Horses for the Souls of Ancestors	141
	すずしろ	Japanese Daikon Radish	129
	すずな	Turnip	129
	せり	Water Dropwort	129
	雑煮	Soup Containing Rice Cakes	127
	素麺	Fine Wheat Noodles	139
た	茅の輪くぐり	Chigaya Ring Passing	136
	粽	Rice Dumpling Wrapped in a Bamboo Leaf	135
	追儺	Scattering Soybeans	130
	月見飾り	Decoration for Moon-viewing	143
	つごもり蕎麦	Soba Noodles Eaten on New Year's Eve	146
	年越し蕎麦	Soba Noodles Eaten on New Year's Eve	146
	屠蘇酒	New Year's Spiced Sake	127

な	なずな	Shepherd's Purse	129
	七草粥	Rice Porridge Containing Seven Kinds of Spring Herbs	128
	願いの糸	Five-colored Threads	139
は	はこべら	Common Chickweed	129
	蛤のお吸い物	Clams in Clear Soup	132
	柊鰯	Decoration for Keeping Away Oni	131
	菱餅	Lozenge-shaped Rice Cake	132
	ひなあられ	Cubic Rice Crackers for the Girl's Doll Festival	132
	ほとけのざ	Nipplewort	129
	雪洞	Classic Candlestand	133
ま	豆まき	Scattering Soybeans	130
	三つ肴	Three Good-luck Foods	126
	水無月	Triangle-shaped Rice Jelly	137
	迎え火	Fire to Welcome the Souls of Ancestors	140

監　修	服部幸應　（はっとり・ゆきお） 学校法人服部学園・服部栄養専門学校理事長・校長。 料理研究家。
イラスト	末吉詠子
翻　訳	高尾桃子
校　正	Casey FARRINGTON
デザイン	奥野正次郎（pororoca）

Editorial Supervision	HATTORI Yukio
Illustration	SUEYOSHI Eiko
Translation	TAKAO Toko
Proofing	Casey FARRINGTON
Design	OKUNO Shojiro (pororoca)

英訳付き ニッポンの名前図鑑　和食・年中行事

2017年 5 月 9 日　初版発行
2021年 4 月14日　4 版発行

編　者	淡交社編集局
発行者	納屋嘉人
発行所	株式会社 淡交社
	本社　〒603-8588 京都市北区堀川通鞍馬口上ル
	営業　075-432-5151　　編集　075-432-5161
	支社　〒162-0061 東京都新宿区市谷柳町39-1
	営業　03-5269-7941　　編集　03-5269-1691
	www.tankosha.co.jp

印刷・製本　三晃印刷株式会社

©2017 淡交社　Printed in Japan
ISBN978-4-473-04181-4

An Illustrated Guide to Japanese Cooking and Annual Events

This book was published in 2017
by TANKOSHA Publishing Co., Ltd.

定価はカバーに表示してあります。落丁・乱丁本がございましたら、小社「出版営業部」宛にお送りください。送料小社負担にてお取り替えいたします。本書のスキャン、デジタル化等の無断複写は、著作権法上での例外を除き禁じられています。また、本書を代行業者等の第三者に依頼してスキャンやデジタル化することは、いかなる場合も著作権法違反となります。